Family Bible Study

THE
Herschel
HOBBS
COMMENTARY

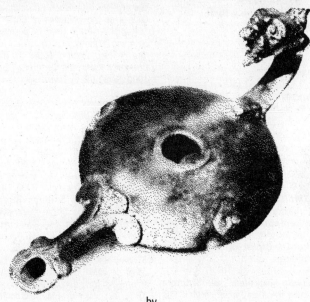

by

Robert J. Dean

WINTER 2002-03
Volume 3, Number 2

GENE MIMS, *President*
LifeWay Church Resources

Ross H. McLaren
Editor-in-Chief

Carolyn Gregory
Copy Editor

Stephen Smith
Graphic Designer

Frankie Churchwell
Technical Specialist

Michael Felder
Lead Adult Ministry Specialist

John McClendon
Mic Morrow
Adult Ministry Specialists

Send questions/comments to
  Editor, *Herschel Hobbs Commentary*
  One LifeWay Plaza
  Nashville, TN 37234-0175
  Or make comments on the web at
  www.lifeway.com

Management Personnel

Louis B. Hanks, *Director*
Publishing
Gary Hauk, *Director*
Adult Ministry Publishing
Bill Craig, *Managing Director*
Adult Ministry Publishing
Alan Raughton, *Director*
Sunday School/Open Group Ministry

ACKNOWLEDGMENTS.–We believe the Bible has God for its author; salvation for its end; and truth, without any mixture of error, for its matter and that all Scripture is totally true and trustworthy. The 2000 statement of *The Baptist Faith and Message* is our doctrinal guideline.

Unless otherwise indicated, all Scripture quotations are from the *King James Version*. This translation is available in a Holman Bible and can be ordered through LifeWay Christian Stores. Scripture quotations identified as CEV are from the *Contemporary English Version.* Copyright © American Bible Society 1991, 1992. Used by permission. Quotations marked HCSB have been taken from the *Holman Christian Standard Bible,* © Copyright 2000 by Broadman & Holman Publishers.

Used by permission. This translation is available in a Holman Bible and can be ordered through LifeWay Christian Stores. Passages marked NASB are from the *New American Standard Bible: 1995 Update.* © The Lockman Foundation, 1960, 1962, 1963, 1968, 1971, 1972, 1973, 1975, 1977, 1995. Used by permission. This translation is available in a Holman Bible and can be ordered through Lifeway Christian Stores. Quotations marked NEB are from *The New English Bible.* Copyright © The Delegates of the Oxford University Press and the Syndics of the Cambridge University Press, 1961, 1970. Reprinted by permission. Quotations marked NIV are from the Holy Bible, *New International Version,* copyright © 1973, 1978, 1984 by International Bible Society (NIVmg. = NIV margin). This translation is available in a Holman Bible and can be ordered through Lifeway Christian Stores. Quotations marked NKJV are from the *New King James Version.* Copyright © 1979, 1980, 1982. Thomas Nelson, Inc., Publishers. Reprinted with permission. This translation is available in a Holman Bible and can be ordered through Lifeway Christian Stores. Quotations marked NRSV are from the *New Revised Standard Version of the Bible,* copyright © 1989 by the Division of Christian Education of the National Council of the Churches of Christ in the United States of America. Used by permission. All rights reserved. Quotations marked REB are from *The Revised English Bible.* Copyright © Oxford University Press and Cambridge University Press, 1989. Reprinted by permission.

The Herschel Hobbs Commentary (ISSN 0191-4219), *Family Bible Study,* is published quarterly by LifeWay Christian Resources of the Southern Baptist Convention, One LifeWay Plaza, Nashville, Tennessee 37234; James T. Draper, Jr., President, and Ted Warren, Executive Vice-President, LifeWay Christian Resources of the Southern Baptist Convention; © Copyright 2002 LifeWay Christian Resources of the Southern Baptist Convention. All rights reserved. Single subscription to individual address, $20.95 per year. If you need help with an order, WRITE LifeWay Church Resources Customer Service, One LifeWay Plaza, Nashville, Tennessee 37234-0113; For subscriptions, FAX (615) 251-5818 or EMAIL subscribe@lifeway.com. For bulk shipments mailed quarterly to one address, FAX (615) 251-5933 or EMAIL CustomerService@lifeway.com. Order ONLINE at www.lifeway.com. Mail address changes to: *The Herschel Hobbs Commentary, Family Bible Study,* One LifeWay Plaza, Nashville, TN 37234-0113.

Printed in the United States of America.

Dedicated in honor of

William Tyndale

1494-1536

Who translated the New Testament into English

and who was working on the Old Testament

when he was put to death for distributing English Bibles.

Contents

Study Theme

Study Theme

Contents

Study Theme

The Bible: God's Book of Grace 97

Study Theme

Christmas: God's Grace Revealed

In *A Christmas Carol*, Charles Dickens told of the transformation of Ebenezer Scrooge from a bitter, selfish, grasping old sinner into a new person. At the end of the book, the author said of Scrooge: "It was always said of him, that he knew how to keep Christmas well, if any man alive possessed the knowledge." Then Dickens added: "May that be truly said of us, and all of us!"[1] How would you describe one who keeps Christmas well?

The overall purpose of this study is to help us celebrate the true meaning of Christmas and to respond in faith and obedience to the Savior, Jesus Christ. This five-session study of the events surrounding the announcement and birth of Jesus Christ is based on the familiar passages from Matthew 1–2 and Luke 1–2. The first session, "Preparing the Way," is the announcement to Zechariah of the forthcoming birth of John the Baptist. The second session, "Using Ordinary People," is based on the announcement to Mary of the impending birth of Jesus. The third session, "Seeking Faithful Obedience," is based on the announcement to Joseph and his obedience in marrying Mary and in caring for her. The fourth session, "Sending the Savior," is based on the announcement of Jesus' birth to the shepherds and their response, including telling others. This is the Evangelism Lesson for the quarter. The fifth session, "Leading to Worship," is based on the coming of the wise men.

This study is designed to help you
- prepare the way for people to believe in Jesus (Dec. 1)
- fulfill the role God has for you in His saving work (Dec. 8)
- obey God always (Dec. 15)
- believe in Jesus and make Him the focus of your Christmas celebration (Dec. 22)
- worship and be devoted to Jesus the Savior (Dec. 29)

Keep in mind the emphasis on praying and giving to international missions during this season.

[1]Charles Dickens, *A Christmas Carol*, in the *Works of Charles Dickens* [New York: Avenel Books, 1978 (1843)], 494.

PREPARING THE WAY

Background Passage: Luke 1:1-25,39-45,57-80
Focal Passage: Luke 1:5-7,11-15a,18-20,68-69,76-79
Key Verse: Luke 1:76

❖ Significance of the Lesson

• The *Theme* of this lesson is that the birth of John the Baptist to an aged, righteous couple revealed God's intention to prepare the way for the Messiah to come into the world.

• The *Life Question* this lesson seeks to address is, How can I know where God is at work in the world?

• The *Biblical Truth* is that God showed through the birth of John the Baptist that He was preparing the way for the coming of the Savior.

• The *Life Impact* is to help you prepare the way for people to believe in Jesus.

The Christmas Season

The prevailing secular worldview prefers the Christmas season to be viewed as a non-religious, end-of-the-year holiday season rather than a celebration of the Savior's birth. Materialistic impulses reach their high points as businesses pin their hopes—and their advertising efforts—on having strong holiday sales. People who live to party see the holidays as a lengthy time for their partying. Many Christians get caught up in this kind of holiday season and miss the opportunities for worship and service that it provides.

In the biblical worldview, God is always at work in the world to complete His redemptive work in Jesus the Savior. God works in and through His people to prepare the hearts of others to believe in Jesus.

Word Study: *Prophet of the Highest*

In Luke 1:76 the word **prophet** is *prophetes,* the normal word for one who was called by God to deliver His word. **Highest** is *hupsistou,* which sometimes refers to the highest place or heaven but usually refers to God Himself. Gabriel told Mary that "the power of the Highest" would "overshadow" her (v. 35). The child who would be conceived would be "the Son of the Highest" (v. 32). After the birth of John the Baptist, Zechariah praised the Lord for his son, who would be **the prophet of the highest** (v. 76; "the Most High," NIV).

❖ Search the Scriptures

Zechariah and Elizabeth were righteous and elderly people who had no children. The angel Gabriel told Zechariah that his prayer had been heard and that his wife would conceive a son. Zechariah asked for a sign that this impossible thing could happen, and Gabriel told Zechariah that he would not be able to speak until the child was born. After the birth of John, the Holy Spirit led Zechariah to use his newly returned voice to praise God for his son and for the greater One whom John would announce.

The four points in the Focal Passage Outline show ways of achieving the Life Impact of preparing others to believe in Jesus.

Keep Your Relationship Growing (Luke 1:5-7)

Why did Luke mention Herod the King? What did he tell us about Zechariah and Elizabeth? Why was childlessness for a married woman a matter for reproach? How did this couple keep their relationship with God and each other growing? When God seems to ignore our prayers, how does this test our faith?

Verses 5-7: **There was in the days of Herod, the king of Judea, a certain priest named Zechariah, of the course of Abia: and his wife was of the daughters of Aaron, and her name was Elizabeth. [6]And they were both righteous before God, walking in all the commandments and ordinances of the Lord blameless. [7]And they had no child, because that Elizabeth was barren, and they both were now well-stricken in years.**

Luke is the only Gospel writer who began with an explanation for how he did his research and writing (vv. 1-4). One of his main concerns was to show the reality and truth of what he wrote. This is one of the reasons that Luke began by mentioning the ruler at the time of the events he was about to record. He mentioned that this took place

in the days of Herod, the king of Judea. Luke did the same thing in 2:1 by listing the rulers when Jesus was born and in 3:1 by listing the rulers when John the Baptist and Jesus began their ministries. Luke rooted these events within the framework of history to ensure that readers knew that he was recording historical events. This was an important way of achieving his objective of showing "the certainty of those things" believed by early Christians (1:4).

Judea was used here by Luke not only of the area in and around Jerusalem but of the land of the Jews, which included Galilee as well as Judea. **Herod** ruled over a territory roughly comparable to the Israel of the time of David's reign. Of course, he was **king** only by permission of the Romans, who had conquered Israel a few years before they gave Herod authority to rule. **Herod** was known in history as Herod the Great, although he was anything but great by God's standards. Herod began to reign in 37 B.C. and ruled until his death in 4 B.C. Since Herod was in his final days when Jesus was born, Jesus' birth was within a few years of 4 B.C., possibly in 7 or 6 B.C.

Another reason Luke mentioned **Herod** was to contrast the lifestyle of the rich and famous with the lifestyle of the people through whom God sent His Son into the world. Herod the Great was a crafty politician and an utterly ruthless man. History shows that the paranoid king killed anyone whom he thought was trying to seize his throne. He put to death some of his sons and even his wife. He was a striking contrast to the old priest and his wife who became the parents of John the Baptist.

Notice how Luke described **Zechariah.** He was **a priest,** but he was not one of the rich and powerful chief priests who ran the temple. Herod ruled over an area that included Galilee, where Mary and Joseph lived and the "hill country" where Zechariah and Elizabeth lived (v. 39). A country preacher is the closest thing in Baptist life to what Zechariah was. He was only one of many priests in the land, and he was not among the prominent ones. His wife **Elizabeth,** as one **of the daughters** or "descendants" (NIV) **of Aaron,** was also from priestly blood. This is one of three facts emphasized in verses 5-7.

Further, **they were both righteous before God, walking in all the commandments and ordinances of the Lord blameless.** They were not righteous in the superficial way of the Pharisees, who were self-righteous. They were righteous in the best sense of Old Testament righteousness. They recognized their need for the mercy of God, and they sought to live in the way that was pleasing to Him.

Blameless does not mean they were sinlessly perfect, but it does mean their faith and lifestyle were pleasing to God.

Zechariah and Elizabeth were the first of six personalities in Luke 1–2 whom God used to perform roles in the coming of Jesus into the world. The others were Mary, Joseph, Simeon, and Anna. None of these six was from among the rich and famous people of the day. Each was from among the common people, but each also was a person of humble faith and true godliness. These were the kind of people through whom God chose to bring His Son into the world.

Zechariah and Elizabeth **had no child, because . . . Elizabeth was barren.** For a Jewish married woman to be barren was considered punishment from God. Elizabeth lived under a cloud of her own disappointment and also the reproach of others. When she later conceived, she praised God for taking away her "reproach" in society (v. 25). To compound the problem, this righteous couple was **well-stricken** ("well along," NIV) **in years.** In some ways they were like Abraham and Sarah, who waited for years for the fulfillment of God's promise of a son. Each passing year made the birth of a child less likely.

No doubt Zechariah and Elizabeth were tempted to lose heart from years of praying with no answer. Yet from verse 13 we learn that their faith had not faltered. They had continued to pray. They maintained their relationship with the Lord and with each other during the long years of waiting and praying. Any personal relationship must be renewed and expressed. This is true of our personal relationship with the Lord, and it is true of human relationships, especially of a husband and a wife.

What are the lasting lessons in verses 5-7?

1. The events of the Christian faith are grounded in the bedrock of history.

2. The people of faith in the Bible were very different from the rich and powerful people of their day.

3. God uses people of genuine faith and godliness in His work.

4. Personal relations with God and with people need to be nurtured and renewed.

Pray Persistently (Luke 1:11-15a)

Why was this the greatest day in Zechariah's life up to that time? Why was he troubled and frightened by the angel? What good news did Gabriel bring? Did Gabriel refer to Zechariah's prayer for a son or for the coming of God's kingdom? Why is Christmas a season of joy? Why is all true prayer persistent?

Verses 11-15a: And there appeared unto him an angel of the Lord standing on the right side of the altar of incense. ¹²And when Zechariah saw him, he was troubled, and fear fell upon him. ¹³But the angel said unto him, Fear not, Zechariah: for thy prayer is heard; and thy wife Elizabeth shall bear thee a son, and thou shalt call his name John. ¹⁴And thou shalt have joy and gladness; and many shall rejoice at his birth. ^{15a}For he shall be great in the sight of the Lord.

Verses 8-10 bridge the gap between verse 7 and verse 11. Zechariah was a member of one of 24 divisions of priests in that day. He was from the division of Abijah [uh-BIGH-juh]. Each division served two weeks per year in the temple, and all divisions served on each of the three main feasts. Priests offered animal sacrifices on the altar of sacrifice, and twice a day during morning and evening sacrifices one priest offered incense on the altar of incense. The temple was a series of courts surrounding the holy place and the holy of holies. The altar of sacrifice was in the court of the priests. The altar of incense was in the holy place. The holy of holies contained the ark of the covenant and was entered only one day a year by the high priest. In the holy place on one side was the table with the showbread, and on the other side was the seven-pronged lampstand. At the back of the holy place, near the curtain into the holy of holies, was the altar of incense. Offering incense signified the prayers of the people. The officiating priest was selected by lot and could serve but once in his lifetime. This was the day when Zechariah served.

Thus this service in the temple was already the high point of Zechariah's life as a priest, but something happened to make it even more important. As Zechariah went about his task, suddenly he saw **an angel of the Lord standing on the right side of the altar of incense**. Zechariah was a godly man, but he was **troubled** and afraid when he saw the angel (whom we later learn was Gabriel). Angels were active in the lives of Bible people, but they seldom appeared in visible form. Thus Zechariah's response was a normal human response.

After trying to reassure the priest with the words **fear not,** the angel delivered his message that Zechariah's **prayer** had been **heard.** Bible students discuss whether the angel was referring to the old couple's prayer for a son or their prayer and the prayer of the people for the coming of the Messiah. Many favor the former view, pointing out that the angel went on to say, **Thy wife Elizabeth shall bear thee a son.** Others point out that as officiating priest for the nation, Zechariah would have been leading in a prayer shared by all the worshipers praying outside the holy place. Actually, both prayers were to be answered. In Zechariah's words of praise after the birth of John, he thanked God for his son and also for the coming of the Son of God, whom his son was to declare. The angel told the priest to name his son **John.** He predicted that his coming would bring **joy and gladness** to Zechariah and that **many** would **rejoice at his birth.** This note of **joy** also is found throughout Luke's account of the birth of Jesus and the events surrounding it. It is an appropriate feeling during the Christian celebration of the birth of the Savior.

Gabriel predicted of John that he would **be great in the sight of the Lord.** He went on to say that John would be filled with the Spirit from birth and that he would turn the hearts of many to God. Verses 15b-17 continue the description of John's mission. He was obviously the prophet like Elijah whom Malachi had foretold (Mal. 4:5-6). His mission was to "make ready a people prepared" for the coming of the Lord (v. 17).

The faithfulness of Zechariah and Elizabeth was expressed in their persistent praying for a son. All true prayer is by nature persistent. This is not because we must convince God of our faith or because we must influence a reluctant God to do our bidding. True prayer is persistent for several reasons. For one thing, since prayer is communion with a personal God, this relationship is expressed over and over. Second, we always have things for which to thank God. Third, real needs in our lives and in the lives of others make it necessary for petitions and intercessions to be expressed repeatedly.

What are the lasting lessons in verses 11-15a?
1. Some days have special significance.
2. God sometimes seems not to answer our prayers right away as we would like.
3. Christmas is a time of joy.
4. True prayer is persistent.

Be Ready to Believe (Luke 1:18-20)

How did Gabriel interpret Zechariah's question? What sign was to be given? How can we explain such doubt by a man of faith? How does our faith equip us to help prepare others to believe?

Verses 18-20: And Zechariah said unto the angel, Whereby shall I know this? for I am an old man, and my wife well-stricken in years. [19]And the angel answering said unto him, I am Gabriel, that stand in the presence of God; and am sent to speak unto thee, and to show thee these glad tidings. [20]And, behold, thou shalt be dumb, and not able to speak, until the day that these things shall be performed, because thou believest not my words, which shall be fulfilled in their season.

Addressing himself to the angel, Zechariah asked a question: **Whereby shall I know this?** ("How can I be sure of this?" NIV; "How will I know that this is so?" NRSV.) Zechariah and his wife had been praying for a child for years. Then when the angel told Zechariah that Elizabeth would conceive and bear a son, the priest asked how this impossible thing could happen. It seemed impossible because, as Zechariah noted, **I am an old man, and my wife well-stricken in years.**

The angel responded to the priest's words **I am an old man** by saying **I am Gabriel.** The angel's description of himself emphasized that he had been sent by God to deliver His message to Zechariah. Only those who are God's most important messengers **stand in the presence of God.** Gabriel implied that Zechariah ought to be overjoyed because he had told him these **glad tidings. Show . . . glad tidings** translates *euangelisasthai,* one of Luke's favorite words for declaring the good news of God.

Gabriel then proceeded to pronounce a judgment on Zechariah. Gabriel told him that he would **not** be **able to speak, until the day that these things shall be performed.** The Lord apparently looked into the heart of Zechariah and saw unbelief and doubt. **Believest not** translates *ouk episteusas,* the usual words for not believing. Notice that Gabriel accused Zechariah of not believing **my words.** Since Gabriel spoke for God, failing to believe his words was the same as not believing God's words.

How could a man of such persistent faith and prayer fail to believe the promise that his prayer was to be answered? Sometimes even people of faith falter in their faith. Zechariah is an example of how a man of faith had a lapse into doubt. Notice several things about Zechariah's doubt and God's response to it. For one thing, Zechariah asked a similar question to that asked by many people of faith: Abraham (Gen. 15:8), Moses (Ex. 4:1-21), and Gideon (Judg. 6:36-40). Each of these men asked questions of the Lord, some of them tinged with doubt.

In other words, people of faith sometimes ask questions of the Lord. Sometimes they even stumble into doubt. However, there are three differences between the occasional doubts of believers and the continuous doubts of unbelievers. (1) Unbelievers usually spread their doubts far and wide. Believers ask God for help. (2) The normal stance for unbelievers is doubt; the normal stance for believers is faith. Doubt is a temporary lapse from which believers move on to stronger faith. The prayer "Lord, I believe; help thou mine unbelief" (Mark 9:24) is a prayer that God will answer. (3) Zechariah asked for a sign. When it was given, he was open to what God said through the sign. When unbelievers ask for signs, they refuse to believe the signs they receive. Thus they continually are asking for more signs (Luke 11:29).

In essence, Zechariah was asking for some sign that the angel's words were true. God sent a sign that was both a sign and a judgment. Zechariah's inability to speak was a sign to him and to others that Gabriel delivered the Lord's true word. When the priest came out to the people and was unable to speak, the people took it as a sign of something unusual (Luke 1:21-22). When Elizabeth conceived, that was further confirmation of the truth of God's promise (vv. 23-25). When Mary visited Elizabeth and the baby stirred in Elizabeth's womb, that was yet another confirmation (v. 44). When Elizabeth's child was born, the neighbors and family were about to name him Zechariah. The mother insisted that the child's name was John. When Zechariah was asked, he wrote, "His name is John" (v. 63). Then Zechariah's speech immediately returned, he was filled with the Spirit, and he praised the Lord for the birth of his son and for the coming of the Savior. All of these things were confirmations, signs, and fulfillments of the promise to Zechariah. He moved from a moment of doubt to greater faith. If we are to influence others to believe, we must be people of faith.

What are the lasting lessons from verses 18-20?

1. Sometimes believers wonder how something impossible will be done.

2. Doubt is normal for unbelievers but should be abnormal for believers.

Look for What God Is Doing (Luke 1:68-69,76-79)

About whom did Zechariah prophesy? What did he say about John? What did he say about the Savior? How did this one old man play a role in God's redemptive plan? How do we determine what God is doing?

Verses 68-69,76-79: Blessed be the Lord God of Israel; for he hath visited and redeemed his people, [69]and hath raised up an horn of salvation for us in the house of his servant David.

. . . .

[76]**And thou, child, shalt be called the prophet of the Highest: for thou shalt go before the face of the Lord to prepare his ways;** [77]**to give knowledge of salvation unto his people by the remission of their sins,** [78]**through the tender mercy of our God; whereby the dayspring from on high hath visited us,** [79]**to give light to them that sit in darkness and in the shadow of death, to guide our feet into the way of peace.**

Zechariah focused his prophecy on the coming One to whom his son would bear witness (vv. 68-69,78-79). He also praised God for his son's unique mission (vv. 76-77). **Blessed be** translates *eulogetos*, a word used in the New Testament only of God and Jesus. **Visited** translates *epeskepsato*, which is used of humans visiting others (Jas. 1:27) and of God's coming to be with and redeem His people (Luke 1:68,78; 7:16). **Horn of salvation** is another Old Testament term fulfilled in the coming of Jesus. Verses 68-69 were obviously spoken of the Savior, for Zechariah mentioned **the house of his servant David.** John, as a son of a priest, was of the tribe of Levi, but Jesus was a descendant of David.

And thou, child was spoken by Zechariah of the miracle child God gave through them in their old age. The importance of John's mission is seen in the words **prophet of the Highest.** As this prophet, John was to **go before the face of the Lord to prepare his ways.** John would not be the Savior, but he would **give knowledge of salvation unto his people.** We know from the later ministry of John the Baptist how he called for repentance, promising **remission of their sins.**

Verses 78-79 return to praise and prophecy concerning the Son of God. His coming would reveal **the tender mercy of . . . God. The dayspring from on high** is one of the Savior's titles. **Dayspring** translates *anatole*, which can mean "east" (Matt. 2:1) or "rising of the sun" (see NIV). The latter seems to fit the context of this passage. The *New Revised Standard Version* and the *Holman Christian Standard Bible* both render it "the dawn from on high." Notice how verse 79 stresses the coming of the **light to them that sit in darkness and in the shadow of death.** "The original metaphor here refers to a party of travellers who, before reaching their destination, have been overtaken by the darkness of a pitch-black night and are now sitting terrified and powerless and expect any moment to be overwhelmed and killed by wild beasts or enemies. But all at once a bright light appears to show them the way, so that they reach their destination safely where they enjoy rest and peace."[1]

God thus gave Zechariah insight into what He was doing in the world and the privilege of being used to do his part in this work. Do we know what God is doing in our world and are we doing our part in this? By comparison to others, Zechariah's part was small, but in God's sight no part is unimportant. Although Zechariah appears only in Luke 1, and although he probably did not live long enough to see the work of his son and the ministry of Jesus, Zechariah did his part.

Godisnowhere. What do you see? *God is nowhere* or *God is now here?* These two sentences use the same letters in the same sequence, but the meanings are the exact opposite of each other. Some people look at the world and their lives and see no evidence of God's hand. Other people look at the world and their lives and see God's hand, hear God's call, and do what they can to advance God's kingdom.

❖ *Spiritual Transformations*

The four outline points show how each believer can prepare others to believe in Jesus. Zechariah and Elizabeth maintained a strong personal relationship with God and with each other, although they were disappointed that they had no children. The angel assured Zechariah that his faithful praying was to be answered in the birth of a son, who would prepare the way for the coming of the Lord. Although Zechariah asked for a sign, the Lord gave a sign that was punishment for his unbelief and a positive sign of the truth of God's word. Zechariah prophesied and praised God for his son and for the One to whom his son would point people.

What actions will you take to achieve each of the following:

Keep your relationship with God vital and up-to-date:

_____

Pray persistently:

_____

Be ready to believe:

_____

Look for what God is doing:

_____

Prayer of Commitment: Lord, help me to be what You want me to be so You can use me to accomplish Your purposes. Amen.

[1]Norval Geldenhuys, *Commentary on the Gospel of Luke*, in the New International Commentary on the New Testament [Grand Rapids: William B. Eerdmans Publishing Company, 1956], 95.

USING ORDINARY PEOPLE

Background Passage: Luke 1:26-56
Focal Passage: Luke 1:26-35,38,46-49
Key Verses: Luke 1:30-31

❖ *Significance of the Lesson*

   • The *Theme* of this lesson is that God revealed to Mary that she would give birth to the Messiah.
   • The *Life Question* addressed by this lesson is, What should I do when God wants to use me in His saving work?
   • The *Biblical Truth* is that through God's power, ordinary people can play significant roles in God's saving work.
   • The *Life Impact* is to help you fulfill the goal God has for you in His saving work.

Doing God's Work

In the secular worldview, voluntary humble service is so rare that individuals who give themselves in unselfish service are recognized as oddities and glaring contradictions to most people's unashamed drive to be served. In addition, a pervasive hunger for the spectacular leaves most people convinced that their service would not make a difference. The secular mind-set also places great value on the rich and famous not on ordinary people. Many professing Christians are content to leave ministry to the professionals.

In the biblical worldview, God accomplishes His work in the world by God's Spirit working effectively in and through ordinary people. Availability is the primary quality needed to be used by God. True believers seek to know and do God's will.

Traditions and Truths About Mary

In the centuries after the time of the apostles, some traditions about Mary developed. Some of these were not consistent with biblical truths about her. She was made into an almost godlike figure through whom and to whom people could pray. They reasoned that since she was the mother of Jesus, who better than she could get His attention and plead their cause? Later traditions claimed that she was sinless and that she remained a virgin throughout her life.

The picture of Mary in the Bible is different from these traditions. Mary was not a channel of grace but a recipient of grace. The Bible presents her as a righteous young woman but makes no claim for her sinlessness. She and Joseph had several children. Although she was the mother of Jesus, she did not govern how He did His mission (see Luke 2:41-52; John 2:1-11). We must not, however, allow ourselves to react so negatively to the false traditions about Mary that we fail to see her as someone whom God used in a special way. God blessed her by calling her to become the mother of Jesus. She is an example of one who did the will of God.

Word Study: *highly favored*

Highly favored in Luke 1:28 translates *kecharitomene.* The related noun is the word for *grace (charis),* which is found in verse 30 as **favor.** Thus the idea in the verb is "to find favor" or "to receive grace." A similar phrase is used in the Old Testament to identify people who found grace in the eyes of the Lord and were thus selected for some special service: Noah (Gen. 6:8), Gideon (Judg. 6:17), and Hannah (1 Sam. 1:18).

❖ Search the Scriptures

When the angel Gabriel told Mary that she was highly favored of the Lord, she was puzzled by what he meant. Gabriel told her that she was to conceive a son whom she was to call Jesus. He was to be the Son of God and the Messiah-King. When Mary asked how this could be, the angel told her that the Holy Spirit would overshadow her and that the child would be the Son of the Most High. After visiting Elizabeth, Mary magnified the Lord for using such an ordinary person as she to accomplish such great things.

The four outline points provide answers to the Life Question: What should I do when God wants to use me in His saving work?

Be Open to Hear from God (Luke 1:26-29)

*When and where did this event take place? What information are we given about Mary? Why was she **troubled**? How was she open to hear from God?*

Verses 26-29: And in the sixth month the angel Gabriel was sent from God unto a city of Galilee, named Nazareth, ²⁷to a virgin espoused to a man whose name was Joseph, of the house of David; and the virgin's name was Mary. ²⁸And the angel came in unto her, and said, Hail, thou that art highly favored, the Lord is with thee: blessed art thou among women. ²⁹And when she saw him, she was troubled at his saying, and cast in her mind what manner of salutation this should be.

The words **in the sixth month** refer to the sixth month of Elizabeth's pregnancy (see vv. 23-25). The place was **a city of Galilee, named Nazareth. The angel Gabriel was sent from God** to deliver a crucial message to **Mary.** Angels are messengers, and no more important message was delivered by any angel. Notice that it was God's message. The appearance of Gabriel to Mary is one of several parallels between the announcement to Mary and Gabriel's appearance to Zechariah.

From our first meeting with Mary, we are told that she was **a virgin.** This is the Greek word *parthenos*, and it refers not to a young woman but specifically to a virgin. Mary indeed was a young woman, probably in her teens. She was **espoused** ("pledged to be married," NIV; "engaged," NRSV, HCSB). Engagements of that day were more binding than ours, and stricter rules were adhered to than in our modern sex-oriented culture. An engagement was entered into by a formal process that could not be broken except by a divorce. An engaged couple did not live together as husband and wife. They did not have sexual relations until after they were married. Thus Mary was still a virgin.

Joseph is introduced as the one to whom Mary was engaged. He was a descendant of David, which was important in establishing Jesus as a descendant of David. Joseph's story is told in Matthew 1:18-25.

Gabriel greeted Mary: **Hail, thou that art highly favored, the Lord is with thee.** In the Word Study we noted that this description of Mary does not mean that she was a source of or channel for grace. Instead, she was a recipient of divine grace and favor.

Like Zechariah, Mary **was troubled.** However, she was troubled more at the message of the angel than at his appearance: "She was much perplexed by his words and pondered what sort of greeting this might be" (NRSV).

Among other things, these verses show a young woman who was open to hear what God wanted to say to her. She was an ordinary person in contrast to the high and mighty of the day. She was not sinless; but like Zechariah and Elizabeth, Mary was a person of true faith and righteousness. When we consider the three of them, we see that the Lord calls old and young people and favors ordinary people of humble faith. This kind of people are open to hear the word of the Lord.

God speaks to us in a variety of ways. He speaks as we read His Word; He speaks as we hear it taught or preached. He often speaks to us through others. Sometimes He speaks in a still small voice within. Sometimes He speaks to us through circumstances. Openness to hear God is a mark of someone whom God can use.

What are the lasting lessons of verses 26-29?

1. God calls ordinary people of humble faith to be used in His saving work.

2. He calls old people and young people.

3. Sometimes people are initially troubled by God's call.

4. To be used by God, people must be open to hear the word of the Lord.

Learn God's Plan (Luke 1:30-33)

How did Gabriel reassure Mary? What message did the angel deliver to Mary? How did Gabriel describe what the child would be and do? How do we learn God's plan for our lives?

Verses 30-33: And the angel said unto her, Fear not, Mary: for thou hast found favor with God. [31]And, behold, thou shalt conceive in thy womb, and bring forth a son, and shalt call his name JESUS. [32]He shall be great, and shall be called the Son of the Highest: and the Lord God shall give unto him the throne of his father David: [33]and he shall reign over the house of Jacob forever; and of his kingdom there shall be no end.

Fear not were the same words that Gabriel had spoken to reassure Zechariah. He called **Mary** by name, thus assuring her that God knew her personally. He repeated that she had **found favor with God.**

Verse 31 was the first clear signal of the extraordinary role that Mary was to play in the saving work of God. She was going to **conceive** and bear **a son.** God told her to call Him **JESUS.** Just as Zechariah had been told the name of his son, so God told Mary the name of her son.

He shall be great are the same words used of John the Baptist (v. 15). However, the greatness of John is not so great as that of Jesus. Jesus would **be called the Son of the Highest.** John was "the prophet of the Highest" (v. 76), but Jesus is **the Son of the Highest.** Jesus also would fulfill the promises of God to **David.** Thus Jesus would be the Messiah-King through whom God would fulfill His promise for a descendant of David to establish an everlasting kingdom: **He shall reign over the house of Jacob forever; and of his kingdom there shall be no end.**

It is not enough to be open to hear God's will. We must learn God's plan and our role in it. This is the second quality needed in order to be used by God in His saving work. After Saul of Tarsus encountered a bright light on the Damascus road, he asked, "Who are you, Lord?" The voice replied, "I am Jesus of Nazareth, whom you are persecuting." Saul asked what amounted to a prayer: "What shall I do, Lord?" (Acts 22:8-10, NIV). God then proceeded to tell him His plan and Saul's part in it. We need to be sensitive to God's plan for this world, and we need to discover His will for our part in His plan.

What are the lasting lessons of verses 30-33?

1. God has a plan of salvation toward which He is moving humanity.
2. He wants people of faith to learn that plan.
3. God has a plan for each life within the larger context of His work of salvation.
4. We need to seek His plan for our lives.

Make a Humble Commitment (Luke 1:34-35,38)

How did Mary's question differ from Zechariah's question? What is the meaning of Gabriel's answer to her? What is the basis for belief in the virgin birth? How is Mary's response a model for all believers?

Verse 34: **Then said Mary unto the angel, How shall this be, seeing I know not a man?**

This verse is another parallel to the announcement to Zechariah (v. 18). Both Zechariah and Mary asked Gabriel similar questions; and although Mary's question was similar in some ways, it was different in other ways. Both questions were asked in response to Gabriel's announcement of conceptions, each of which was miraculous in its own way. The first conception was to an elderly couple, and thus it was not as miraculous as a conception by a virgin; however, it was considered miraculous by Zechariah. Both Zechariah and Mary asked how these conceptions were to take place, but Zechariah asked for some assurance that such a miracle was possible. Mary did not question the possibility; instead, she asked about the process. "She does not ask for a sign to prove the truth of the words, but asks for further information. She believes that what he has declared as God's messenger is going to happen. But she does not understand how it will be realized, and therefore asks: 'How shall this be, seeing I know not a man?'"[1]

What was in Mary's mind when she asked this question? Some believe that she may have thought that the child was to be born after she was married to Joseph. Others insist that she understood from the first that this was to be a miraculous conception to a virgin. They point out that she would not have asked the question if she thought He was to be conceived in the usual way.

Verse 35: **And the angel answered and said unto her, The Holy Ghost** [Spirit] **shall come upon thee, and the power of the Highest shall overshadow thee: therefore also that holy thing which shall be born of thee shall be called the Son of God.**

Gabriel's answer clearly showed that it was to be a miraculous conception and that the child would be born to a virgin. The overshadowing presence of God's Spirit would cause Mary to conceive a son. **Overshadow** is the language of divine creation and has none of the sexual overtones of gods having sexual intercourse with humans, which was common in the pagan myths of that day.

Gabriel further told Mary, **That holy thing** ("holy one," NIV) **which shall be born of thee shall be called the Son of God.** Strictly speaking, the miracle was in the conception to a virgin. Once conceived the child grew normally within the womb and was born in the usual way. However, the child was born to a virgin. Thus we refer to it as the virgin birth. Some people claim to have trouble believing this miracle. Some who deny the virgin birth deny all miracles; therefore, their denial of this miracle is no surprise. They believe that this is a universe that developed in purely natural ways and that it is governed by purely natural laws. Thus supernatural things are automatically excluded.

Those of us who believe the miracle of divine creation and salvation because we have experienced the hand of God on our lives have little trouble believing the miracles of the Bible.

A skeptical physician asked a Christian friend if he would believe an unmarried mother who claimed that her child had no father. The Christian answered: "If her son had been born in answer to prophecy for 1,500 years; if angels had sung at His birth; if He had lived a sinless life, cleansed lepers, and raised the dead; if men had crucified Him and the sun hid its face in shame; if He had been raised from the dead and ascended up to heaven; and if He had blessed the world for 20 centuries—like One who was born of a virgin—oh, yes, doctor, I would believe her story."

Herschel Hobbs pointed out that Luke was a physician (Col. 4:14). Hobbs wrote: "Everything in Luke's training would lead him to doubt such a story. To record it would subject him to criticism by his colleagues. Yet having traced all things accurately, Luke was so convinced of its truth that he boldly and beautifully penned the most complete account of the virgin birth of Jesus on record. His record is the greatest proof of the virgin birth both historically and scientifically."[2]

Others claim to believe some Bible miracles but not this one. Some doubt this miracle because it is mentioned in the Bible only in the birth narratives of Matthew and Luke. Believers ask how often must a miracle be mentioned in God's Word. Critics point out that the evangelistic sermons of the Book of Acts do not mention the virgin birth. The apostles focused on the cross and resurrection of Jesus. This, however, does not cast doubt on the virgin birth.

Still others deny the virgin birth because they say that it denies the humanity of Jesus. However, as already noted, the child developed normally following the miraculous conception. Some pagan gods sprang full grown into the world. Jesus was miraculously conceived, but He was born and grew up as a human being. He was fully divine and fully human.

Verse 38: And Mary said, Behold the handmaid of the Lord; be it unto me according to thy word. And the angel departed from her.

Gabriel strengthened Mary by telling her of Elizabeth's conception in her old age (v. 36). Then he reminded her, "With God nothing shall be impossible" (v. 37).

Verse 38 presents Mary's humble commitment of faith and obedience. Mary referred to herself as **the handmaid of the Lord.** She saw herself as a servant of the Lord who was ready to do whatever He wanted her to do or be whatever He wanted her to be. She had heard God's **word** and was ready to abide by it. Thus she said, "May it be to me as you have said" (NIV).

Mary did not ask any other questions, although she must have had some important ones. For example, she must have wondered how this would affect her marriage. How would it affect her reputation in the community and even within her family? If she had such questions, she did not ask them. When God revealed His will to Mary, she committed herself to God. She trusted God to fulfill His word in His own way. This kind of faith is inherent in the kind of commitment she made to the Lord.

Humble commitment is always a crucial step in finding and doing the will of God for our lives. God does not show us all the future steps in our journey. He merely calls us to hear and obey. Commitment is the bridge between hearing and obeying. Mary's was a unique calling. Only she was ever called to be the mother of Jesus, the Son of God. However, each of us has a role to play in God's saving work. When we are open to His will, He shows us what our role is. Then we must humbly commit ourselves to Him, allowing Him to use us in whatever way is needed.

What are the lasting lessons in verses 34-35,38?

1. God hears and answers questions of honest believers.

2. God is able to use His miraculous power to accomplish His work.

3. Jesus was conceived by the Holy Spirit and born to a virgin named Mary.

4. We should humbly commit ourselves to do our individual parts in God's saving work.

Express Grateful Praise (Luke 1:46-49)

What happened between verses 38 and 46? For what did Mary praise God? What did she mean about future generations calling her blessed?

Verses 46-49: And Mary said, My soul doth magnify the Lord, 47and my spirit hath rejoiced in God my Savior. 48For he hath regarded the low estate of his handmaiden: for, behold, from hence-forth all generations shall call me blessed. 49For he that is mighty hath done to me great things; and holy is his name.

After Gabriel's appearance, Mary made a trip to visit her relative Elizabeth. This involved a journey from Nazareth to the hill country of Judea. Elizabeth was six months pregnant at the time. Elizabeth's words reinforced the message already delivered by Gabriel. When she saw Mary, the baby inside her leaped. She blessed Mary as the one who would be the mother of the Lord Jesus. Mary responded with powerful words of praise to God.

Mary magnified and praised the Lord. She rejoiced in Him and in what He was going to do through her and through the One to whom she would give birth. The theme of her praises was the way in which the Lord used the humble and lowly to accomplish His great purposes. She mentioned herself as an example. She spoke of the Lord's concern for **the low estate of his handmaiden.** Yet God was going to do **great things** through her. And future **generations** would **call** her **blessed.**

Since this verse and similar words by Elizabeth—Elizabeth's words in verse 42 have been made into a prayer invoking Mary's help in times of need—often are used to support the idea of Mary as a mediator with God and Jesus, we need to note their true meaning. Mary was not boasting when she said that **all generations** would call her **blessed.** She was humbly acknowledging the great privilege that God had given her to be the mother of the Messiah. Elizabeth's words in verse 42 should be understood in the same way. She said to Mary, "Blessed art thou among women, and blessed is the fruit of thy womb." Every pious Jewish girl hoped that she would be the mother of the Messiah, and Mary was to receive that blessing. The emphasis in verse 42 is on Jesus more than on Mary. The greatness of a Jewish mother was judged by her children. Judged by Jesus, Mary was indeed blessed. Elizabeth also called Mary "the mother of my Lord" (v. 43). This is not the same thing as calling Mary the queen of heaven and the mother of God. It is a joyous recognition that Mary was to be the one whom God chose to bear and give birth to His Son, our Lord. Our last picture of Mary in the Bible is as one of the believers praying together prior to the day of Pentecost (Acts 1:14).

The positive message of verses 46-49 in this lesson is as an example of how a believer responds to God when He reveals His will and how a believer commits to do His will. We give praise to God for allowing us to be used by Him in His saving work. None of us is called to do what Mary did, but each of us has a distinctive calling for which we too should praise the Lord.

What are the lasting lessons in verses 46-49?

1. Those who are called to do God's work do not take the credit to themselves.

2. Those who are called to do God's work praise the Lord for His use of them.

❖ *Spiritual Transformations*

God sent Gabriel to tell Mary that she was highly favored of the Lord. Gabriel told her that she was to have a child who would be the Son of God and the Messiah. When Mary asked about having a child since she was a virgin, Gabriel told her that the Holy Spirit would over-shadow her and that the child would be the Son of God. Mary humbly surrendered herself to be used by God. After her visit with Elizabeth, Mary praised the Lord for using such a lowly person in this great way.

How can we know and do the will of God? This lesson gives four answers from the example of God's dealings with Mary. We must be open to the revelation of His will. We must be willing to learn how our part fits into His larger plan. We must humbly commit to be used by Him according to His will. We should praise Him for allowing us to be used in His saving work.

Ask yourself about your life in these four areas:

Am I open to hear what God wants me to do? _____

Do I know my part in God's larger plan? _____

Am I humbly committed to do His will? _____

Am I praising Him for using me in His work? _____

Prayer of Commitment: Lord, above all things else, I want to be used by You in Your saving work. Show me Your will and help me to do it. Amen.

[1]Geldenhuys, *Commentary on the Gospel of Luke,* 76.

[2]Herschel H. Hobbs, *An Exposition of the Gospel of Luke* [Grand Rapids: Baker Book House, 1966], 33.

SEEKING FAITHFUL OBEDIENCE

Background Passage: Matthew 1:18-25; 2:13-23
Focal Passage: Matthew 1:18-25; 2:13-15,19-23
Key Verse: Matthew 1:24

❖ *Significance of the Lesson*

• The *Theme* of this lesson is that God instructed Joseph to marry Mary, and Joseph obeyed.
• The *Life Question* this lesson seeks to address is, What does it mean to obey God?
• The *Biblical Truth* is that obeying God requires faith and courage, and it is always the right and best thing to do.
• The *Life Impact* is to help you obey God always.

Obeying God

The prevailing secular mind-set scoffs at the idea of looking to a higher authority for guidance in making decisions. The idea of praying about matters such as whom to marry, where to work, or where to live is viewed as a copout rather than as a strong character trait. In this mind-set, obedience sounds like something for the meek and helpless rather than for the proud and free.

In the biblical worldview, God helps people discover what He wants them to do, and He provides motivation and strength to do His will. Obeying God isn't always easy, but it is the right thing to do.

Joseph—Model of Obedience

Did you realize that the New Testament does not contain anything that Joseph ever said? Surely he spoke, but his words are not found in the Bible. Instead, the Bible tells us what he did. Joseph was consistently a person who obeyed God. He obeyed God when he married Mary after she was pregnant with Jesus, the Son of God. He did not consummate the marriage until after the birth of Jesus. When an angel warned him of danger to Jesus, Mary, and himself, Joseph obeyed and went immediately to Egypt. When God told Joseph to return to Judea, he went; then he went on to Nazareth when God sent further instructions. "We may call him 'Quiet Joseph.' His hallmark is obedience—prompt, simple, and unspectacular obedience. And in this sense Joseph prefigures the Gospel of Matthew's understanding of righteousness: to be righteous is simply to obey the Word of God; righteousness is, simply, to *do*—a favorite word in this Gospel—what God has said."[1]

Word Study: *just*

Dikaios is the Greek word for **just** in Matthew 1:19. In the New Testament, it refers to a person who is right with God and whose life as a result is a life of righteousness. A just person trusts in and is obedience to God. Being just includes practicing both justice and mercy.

❖ *Search the Scriptures*

Joseph planned to divorce his fiancee Mary when he discovered that she was going to have a child. An angel of the Lord explained to him that the child was conceived by the Holy Spirit and told him that the child would be the incarnate Savior from sin. When Joseph was told to marry Mary, he obeyed. After the coming of the wise men, Joseph was warned to flee the wicked Herod; and Joseph immediately took his family to Egypt. After Herod died, God led Joseph to head home and led him to Nazareth because Archelaus [ahr-kuh-LAY-uhs], Herod's evil son, reigned in Judea.

The four points of the Focal Passage Outline answer the Life Question, What does it mean to obey God?

Face Unexpected Events Graciously (Matt. 1:18-19)

Who is the main person in Matthew 1–2? What was the marital status of Joseph? How did he find out that Mary was going to have a child? What were his options? What decision did he make? What does this reveal about Joseph?

1:18-19: Now the birth of Jesus Christ was on this wise: When as his mother Mary was espoused to Joseph, before they came

together, she was found with child of the Holy Ghost [Spirit].
**¹⁹Then Joseph her husband, being a just man, and not willing to
make her a public example, was minded to put her away privily.**

Although this lesson focuses on lessons we learn from Joseph, Jesus
is the main person in all of the birth narratives. The first part of verse
18 points to **the birth of Jesus Christ** ("this is how the birth of Jesus
Christ came about," NIV). The first two chapters of Matthew and Luke
tell of the roles of others, such as Zechariah, Elizabeth, Mary, Joseph,
the shepherds, and the wise men; however, these were only human
players in the event of God's sending His Son into the world.

Jewish marriages in that day consisted of three stages:
(1) the agreement to be married, which was often made by fathers
when their children were young; (2) the betrothal, which was a formal
binding pledge made by the man and the woman; and (3) the marriage, after which the husband and wife lived together as a married
couple. **Mary** and **Joseph** were in the second stage. They were
espoused ("engaged," NRSV, HCSB; "betrothed," NASB; "pledged to be
married," NIV). Although Mary is called the **mother** of Jesus, He had
not yet been born. Joseph is called **her husband,** but they had not yet
actually been married. The event in the Focal Passage took place
before they came together. Their betrothal stage had strong legal
responsibilities and could be ended only by a divorce.

Mary had been with Elizabeth for three months (Luke 1:56). After
Mary returned to Nazareth, **she was found with child.** This does not
imply that Mary had tried to hide this from Joseph, but it merely
states that at some point he found out about her pregnancy. Did Mary
try to tell Joseph of her experience with the angel Gabriel? There is no
indication that she did. She probably trusted God to reveal this miracle to Joseph if that was His will. To do so called for great faith on her
part, because when the people of Nazareth realized Mary was to bear
a child outside of marriage, this would have been considered
scandalous behavior.

This is apparently what Joseph believed. As the man to whom she
was betrothed, he had two options. One was that he could marry her,
even though he thought the child had been fathered by another man.
This did not seem a good option since Mary seemed to have been
unfaithful and thus to have rejected him and his love. His other option
was to divorce her. The divorce could have been done in two ways. One
way would have been to divorce her in a public way designed to shame

and embarrass her. This action would also show that Joseph had not had sexual relations with his betrothed, which in the minds of the people in that day—and by biblical standards—was sinful. The other way to divorce Mary was to do it privately, calling as little attention as possible to the divorce. This way would shield Mary from some of the gossip; at least, Joseph would not be a party to shaming her.

Matthew explained what this decision showed about Joseph. He was **a just man. Just** translates *dikaios*, which is usually translated "righteous" (NIV, HCSB). The same Greek word is used to describe Zechariah and Elizabeth in Luke 1:6. Sometimes this word was used to describe a person who was just in a legalistic way. If that merely were Matthew's meaning, Joseph would have demanded that Mary be punished to the full limit of the law. But the word has another dimension. When Jesus defined *righteousness* in the Sermon on the Mount, He said that the righteousness of kingdom citizens must be different from that of the scribes and Pharisees (Matt. 5:20). He then proceeded to set forth a way of righteousness that includes love and mercy as well as upholding the highest moral standards (vv. 21-48). Joseph chose to act mercifully instead of legalistically. By planning to divorce Mary quietly, Joseph showed mercy toward her.

Mary's pregnancy was a surprise to Joseph. We are not told how he felt when he first heard this news. We can only guess how he felt. Perhaps he was angry; surely he was disappointed. But whatever Joseph may have felt, he acted with righteousness and mercy. He acted graciously. All of us at times face unexpected events, some of them traumatic. We do not control most of the things that happen to us. We are accountable for how we respond. How do you respond at such times? Do you act in a gracious way?

What are the lasting lessons in verses 18-19?

1. Sometimes we experience unexpected and traumatic events.
2. We should face such situations with grace.

Trust God's Word Courageously (Matt. 1:20-25)

How did Joseph find out the nature of the child to be born? What did the Lord tell him to do? What things about the child were revealed to Joseph? How did Joseph respond to what God told him to do?

1:20-23: But while he thought on these things, behold, the angel of the Lord appeared unto him in a dream, saying, Joseph, thou son

of David, fear not to take unto thee Mary thy wife: for that which is conceived in her is of the Holy Ghost [Spirit]. **21And she shall bring forth a son, and thou shalt call his name JESUS: for he shall save his people from their sins. 22Now all this was done, that it might be fulfilled which was spoken of the Lord by the prophet, saying, 23Behold, a virgin shall be with child, and shall bring forth a son, and they shall call his name Emmanuel, which being interpreted is, God with us.**

The Lord had told Mary about the virgin birth by sending the angel Gabriel to her. God spoke to Joseph when **the angel of the Lord appeared unto him in a dream.** One of Matthew's purposes in writing was to emphasize that Jesus was the Messiah from the line of David; thus the angel addressed Joseph as **thou son of David.** The heart of the angel's message was the command for Joseph **to take . . . Mary** to be his **wife.** This had been an option all along, but now it became a command when the Lord revealed to Joseph that the child **conceived in her is of the Holy Ghost.**

Verse 20 is similar to Luke 1:35, where Gabriel told Mary essentially the same thing. The child was miraculously conceived to a virgin by the Holy Spirit. Some people claim that people of the first century were gullible about miracles because they were ignorant of scientific natural laws, but Mary and Joseph knew that a virgin did not conceive a child without a human father. This was a unique miracle, and they believed the word of the Lord.

The angel revealed to Joseph some key truths about the miracle child. Just as Gabriel told Mary to name the child Jesus, so the angel told Joseph the same thing. However, the angel told Joseph the reason for this name: **Call his name JESUS, for he shall save his people from their sins.** The name **JESUS** is the same as the Hebrew *Joshua.* Both names mean "the Lord saves." Many Jews were looking for a savior from the Romans, but Jesus was to save His people from a far worse and more basic plight—sin.

Matthew 1–2 emphasizes that Jesus fulfilled Old Testament Scriptures. The angel told Joseph that Jesus would fulfill the prophecy of Isaiah 7:14 concerning the virgin birth. The name of this virgin-born One was to be **Emmanuel, which being interpreted is, God with us.** This is a reference to the unique miracle of the nature of Jesus as the divine-human Son of God. God came to be among human beings as a human being, while remaining the Son of God. We call this the incarnation. The virgin birth is a sign of the reality and significance of this doctrine.

1:24-25: **Then Joseph being raised from sleep did as the angel of the Lord had bidden him, and took unto him his wife: ²⁵and knew her not till she had brought forth her firstborn son: and he called his name JESUS.**

A key word in the events of Joseph's part in the birth of Jesus is **did.** After he woke up from sleeping and seeing the angel in his dreams, he **did as the angel of the Lord had bidden him.** Joseph accepted by faith that the angel had delivered God's message. He believed what the angel had said, and he obeyed the command to take Mary as his **wife.**

This was an act of faith and courage. By marrying Mary, he shielded her from some of the gossip. Joseph thus acted with courage because he would become the focus for some of the slander. Herschel Hobbs wrote: "Under the lash of public scorn Mary's tender flesh would quiver. But always between her and the lash stood Joseph. His strength became her strength. Surely God in omniscience chose her who was to be the mother of his Son. But with equal wisdom He placed His hand upon him who was to be His foster-father."²

The word **knew** is used in the Bible to describe the most intimate of human knowledge of another person—sexual union. Thus although Joseph married Mary as soon as possible, he did not have sexual relations with her until after Jesus' birth. The use of the words **till** and **firstborn** strongly imply that after Jesus' birth Mary and Joseph lived together as husband and wife and had children of their own. This is confirmed by passages such as 13:55-56 and Mark 6:3. As a further act of obedience to the angel's message, Joseph named the child **JESUS.**

Three characteristics of Joseph are highlighted in verses 20-25: trust, courage, and obedience. Joseph showed trust in believing the message of God through the angel. Believing that the Holy Spirit conceived the child took great faith. Marrying Mary took courage. In all his actions Joseph obeyed the Lord. He was sensitive to what the Lord said to him.

What lasting lessons are found in verses 20-25?

1. We should be sensitive to what the Lord is saying to us.
2. We should believe His word.
3. Jesus is the divine-human Son of God and the Savior from sin.

4. We should obey God without question or objection.

5. We should be courageous in doing God's will.

Heed God's Warnings Immediately (Matt. 2:13-15)

*Who were **they** referred to in verse 13? How did God communicate with Joseph? When did Joseph obey the message from the Lord?*

2:13-15: And when they were departed, behold, the angel of the Lord appeareth to Joseph in a dream, saying, Arise, and take the young child and his mother, and flee into Egypt; and be thou there until I bring thee word: for Herod will seek the young child to destroy him. [14]When he arose, he took the young child and his mother by night, and departed into Egypt: [15]and was there until the death of Herod: that it might be fulfilled which was spoken of the Lord by the prophet, saying, Out of Egypt have I called my son.

They in verse 13 refers to the wise men, whose story is told in verses 1-12. The deceitful Herod had tried to use them to bring him information where Jesus was, but the Lord warned them of Herod's evil intent and they left the country without Herod's knowledge. God knew the evil heart of Herod and knew what he would do when he found that the wise men had seen through his scheme. Thus God sent **the angel of the Lord** again **to Joseph in a dream.** This seems to have been the usual way God communicated with this godly man.

This time the message was an urgent warning. God told Joseph to get up **and take the young child and his mother, and flee into Egypt.** The reason for haste was that **Herod** would **seek the young child to destroy him.** Anyone in that day would have no trouble believing this warning. Herod had killed members of his own family whom he suspected of plotting to seize his throne. He would have no qualms about killing a young child. As verses 16-18 show, Herod was willing to slaughter all the boy babies in Bethlehem in order to kill the One whom the wise men called the "king of the Jews."

God told Joseph to **flee into Egypt.** There were many Jews in Egypt in that day, so Mary, Joseph, and Jesus could find a temporary home there. Joseph was told to stay in Egypt until the Lord sent word for them to leave sometime after the **death of Herod.**

The last part of verse 15 is a quotation of Hosea 11:1. It draws a parallel between the Israelites' deliverance from Egypt and the protection and return of Jesus from Egypt. "Just as God brought the nation of Israel out of Egypt to inaugurate his original covenant with them, so again God is bringing the Messiah, who fulfills the hopes of Israel, out of Egypt as he is about to inaugurate his new covenant."[3]

Joseph picked up the sense of urgency from the angel's words. Thus he did not wait until morning. Instead, **he arose, he took the young child and his mother by night, and departed into Egypt.** Again there is no record of anything Joseph said. His actions speak louder than any words. Recruits in the military are trained to obey a command without delay. Joseph believed that the angel spoke of a danger that could not be avoided except by immediate action. Therefore, he acted.

The word **departed** in verses 13 and 14 is *anachoreo.* It is used here and elsewhere in Matthew to convey the idea of withdrawal from danger (see 4:12 and 12:15).

What are some of the lasting lessons in verses 13-15?

1. Sometimes God's commands call for immediate action.

2. When God calls us to obey immediately, we should obey without delay.

Follow God's Directions Consistently (Matt. 2:19-23)

How did Herod die? How did the Lord communicate with Joseph? What did He tell him to do? What danger did Joseph foresee in obeying the first command? Why was the command later altered about his ultimate destination? Why was this change made?

2:19-23: **But when Herod was dead, behold, an angel of the Lord appeareth in a dream to Joseph in Egypt, [20]saying, Arise, and take the young child and his mother, and go into the land of Israel: for they are dead which sought the young child's life. [21]And he arose, and took the young child and his mother, and came into the land of Israel. [22]But when he heard that Archelaus did reign in Judea in the room of his father Herod, he was afraid to go thither: notwithstanding, being warned of God in a dream, he turned aside into the parts of Galilee: [23]and he came and dwelt in a city called Nazareth: that it might be fulfilled which was spoken by the prophets, He shall be called a Nazarene.**

Finally the news arrived that the wicked **Herod was dead.** Flavius Josephus, a first-century Jewish historian, is our source for documenting many of the evil things that Herod did. Although Josephus did not tell of the slaughter in Bethlehem, he told of many other acts of terror. Josephus also told how Herod died a painful death. As Herod was dying, he realized that the Jews would celebrate his death. Therefore, he came up with a plan designed to ensure mourning at his death. He gave orders that a number of Jews were to be killed when he died. Fortunately, these orders were never carried out.

Once again **an angel of the Lord** appeared **in a dream to Joseph.** God told him to take his family and return to **the land of Israel.** He was told **they are dead which sought the young child's life.** Joseph obeyed and brought his family **into the land of Israel.** However, some changes in government positions had happened after Herod's will took force. Galilee as well as Judea had been under Herod's control. But at his death his kingdom was divided among four of his sons. **Archelaus** [ahr-kuh-LAY-uhs] ruled **in Judea.** His reputation was similar to that of his father's. Therefore, Joseph **was afraid to go** there. Joseph's view of the danger was reinforced by another message from God: "Having been warned in a dream, he withdrew to the district of Galilee" (NIV).

Bible students offer varying interpretations of the words **that it might be fulfilled which was spoken by the prophets, He shall be called a Nazarene.** This exact quotation is not found in the Old Testament. There are two main views. Perhaps Matthew was alluding to Isaiah 1:11, where the Messiah is described as a "branch" or "shoot" (*neser,* hence **Nazarene**) from the root of Jesse. This was the view of Herschel Hobbs. Another possibility is that Matthew did not intend to refer to a specific prophetic quotation. R. T. France explained: "The formula introducing the quotation differs from the regular pattern in two ways: it refers not to a single prophet but to **the prophets,** and it concludes not with 'saying' *(legontos)* but with 'that' *(hoti).* This suggests that it is not meant to be a quotation of a specific passage, but a summary of a theme of prophetic expectation. Thus it has been suggested that Matthew saw in the obscurity of Nazareth the fulfilment of Old Testament indications of a humble and rejected Messiah; for Jesus to be known by the derogatory epithet *Nazoraios* (see John 1:46) was not compatible with the expected royal dignity of the Messiah."[4]

What are the lasting lessons of verses 19-23?

1. God continues to give guidance to His obedient servants.
2. Faithful servants consistently obey God and follow His guidelines.

❖ *Spiritual Transformations*

Joseph's primary part in God's work is recorded in Matthew 1–2. He was not a major ongoing figure in the biblical story; however, he played a key role in protecting Jesus and Mary during the early hazardous period. Joseph was a righteous man who showed mercy toward Mary, whom he originally thought had sinned against him. He showed trust in believing what the angel told him concerning the miracle of Jesus, and He showed courage in marrying Mary. Joseph immediately obeyed the Lord's warning when Herod was trying to destroy Jesus. He consistently followed God's directions in returning from Egypt and settling in Nazareth. The last mention of Joseph in the life of Jesus is the visit to the temple when Jesus was 12 years old (Luke 2:41-52). Apparently Joseph died before Jesus began His public ministry, but the actions of this quiet man of faith and courage were essential in the early days. He no doubt helped Jesus during his growing up years also. Jesus was called "the carpenter's son" (Matt. 13:55) and "the carpenter" (Mark 6:3). Joseph was His teacher in this and other things during those years.

This lesson is designed to help you obey God in all kinds of situations. How well do you obey God in each of the following situations?

Unexpected events bring you disappointment and pain. _____

_____

God calls you to do something that is far bigger than you can achieve without His miraculous power. _____

_____

God calls you to act with courage in a dangerous situation. _____

_____

God calls you to do something urgent. _____

_____

Prayer of Commitment: Lord, help me to obey You with grace, trust, courage, urgency, and consistency. Amen.

[1]Frederick Dale Bruner, *The Christbook: Matthew 1–12* [Waco: Word Book Publishers, 1987], 36.

[2]Herschel H. Hobbs, *An Exposition of the Gospel of Matthew,* [Grand Rapids: Baker Book House, 1965], 19.

[3]Craig L. Blomberg, "Matthew," in *The New American Commentary,* vol. 22 [Nashville: Broadman Press, 1992], 67.

[4]R. T. France, *The Gospel According to Matthew,* in The Tyndale New Testament Commentaries [Grand Rapids: William B. Eerdmans Publishing Company, 1997], 88.

SENDING THE SAVIOR

Background Passage: Luke 2:1-20
Focal Passage: Luke 2:8-20
Key Verse: Luke 2:11

❖ *Significance of the Lesson*

• The *Theme* of this lesson is that God revealed to the shepherds that the Messiah had been born in Bethlehem.

• The *Life Question* this lesson seeks to address is, How does the celebration of Christmas involve me?

• The *Biblical Truth* is that the message that God sent Jesus to be the Savior is good news for all people.

• The *Life Impact* is to help you believe in Jesus and make Him the focus of your celebration of Christmas.

• This is the *Evangelism Lesson* for this quarter.

Holiday or Holy Day?

In the secular worldview, Jesus' birth is unimportant. If it actually occurred at all, it was nothing more than the birth of another figure of history. Secular-minded people celebrate the holiday season, but it is a celebration of time off from work, indulgence in materialism, and participation in parties.

In the biblical worldview, Jesus' birth has eternal implications. His birth signals God's acting to redeem people from their sins. God fulfilled His promises of a Savior and graciously offered salvation to all people who will put their faith in Jesus. Christmas is the celebration of God's priceless gift of Himself.

Word Study: *Savior*

The Greek word *soter* is used in Luke 2:11 for **Savior.** It is related to the words for "save" *(sozo)* and "salvation" *(soteria)*. In ancient times *soter* often was used of a human ruler who was considered a benefactor, deliverer, or preserver. It was also freely applied to pagan gods. The Jews used it as a title for God in the Old Testament. By the first century, the Jews, after centuries of persecution, were looking for a savior who would deliver them from their enemies. But some Jews and many Gentiles also were hungering for a Savior who would conquer the real enemies of humanity—sin and death. This is what Jesus the Savior came to do.

❖ *Search the Scriptures*

On the night of Jesus' birth in Bethlehem, an angel revealed to shepherds that the Savior had been born. Jesus also was revealed to be the One who meant glory for God and peace for humanity. Invited to come and see Him, the shepherds went, saw for themselves, and went out to tell others.

The three points of the Focal Passage Outline are designed to help you experience the Life Impact of believing in Jesus and making Him the focus of your Christmas celebration.

Hear the Good News (Luke 2:8-12)

*What is the significance of the first announcement of Jesus' birth being made to shepherds? What is the significance of the message being delivered by an angel? Why was the angel's message **good tidings of great joy**? What is the meaning of each of the titles of the One who was born? What sign was given to the shepherds to help them find Jesus?*

Verses 8-10: And there were in the same country shepherds abiding in the field, keeping watch over their flock by night. [9]And, lo, the angel of the Lord came upon them, and the glory of the Lord shone round about them: and they were sore afraid. [10]And the angel said unto them, Fear not: for, behold, I bring you good tidings of great joy, which shall be to all people.

Henry Law said, "In Christ Jesus heaven meets earth and earth ascends to heaven."[1] Events surrounding the birth of Jesus and the birth itself show the truth of this insight. We see heaven meeting earth in several ways. For one thing, the appearances of angels to Zechariah, Mary, Joseph, and the shepherds show how messengers from God came from heaven to deliver God's messages to those involved in these miraculous events. The earthly side of these angelic announcements is seen in the people to whom they delivered the messages. Those who received the messages were not the rich and famous of the day; they were ordinary people, usually relatively poor people.

Another example of the truth of Law's words is the miraculous conception or virgin birth. The Gospels of Matthew and Luke emphasize that Mary was a virgin when she conceived and when she gave birth. This shows heaven meeting earth as Jesus was conceived by the Holy Spirit in a virgin. The human side of this is seen in the fact that the child who was conceived by the Spirit grew and was born as a human baby. Another aspect of the earthly side of this was the humble circumstances of the birth of the eternal Word when He became flesh.

In the same country ("region," NASB) refers to a place near ("nearby," NIV) Bethlehem, where Jesus had been born. **Shepherds** were doing what shepherds do. They were **in the field, keeping watch over their flock.** Herschel Hobbs pointed out that we don't really know the date of Jesus' birth—either the year or the day. "The fact that the sheep were in the fields suggests a time between March and November, the time when they were kept out in the open."[2]

The strange events about to happen to the shepherds took place at **night.** Most people looked down on shepherds. Some people even thought of them not only as lower-class but also as dishonest. Other Bible students agree that shepherds were lower class, but these Bible students point to the positive reputation of shepherds in the Bible. David was a shepherd. Jesus is the good Shepherd. In either case, shepherds were certainly not the kind of people to whom an earthly king or emperor would announce the birth of a newborn king. Yet the shepherds were the first group to hear the good news of the Savior's birth.

An **angel of the Lord** made the momentous announcement. Luke wrote that the angel **came upon them** ("appeared to them," NIV; "stood before them," NASB). When this happened, **the glory of the Lord shone round about them. The glory of the Lord** in the Old Testament was the majestic presence of the Lord. **Shone** indicates that the appearance involved a bright light.

The normal reaction for most people at such a time was the response of the shepherds—**they were sore afraid. Sore afraid** is a combination of two Greek words for fear—*ephobethesan phobon*—together with the word "great" *(megan).* This combination literally means "to fear with a great fear." It can be translated "terribly frightened" (NASB) or "terrified" (NIV, HCSB). This response is similar to that of Zechariah's (1:12). The same kind of fear probably was the experience of each one who saw and heard an angel. At least, the typical response of the angel was **fear not** (see 1:13,30; Matt. 1:20).

We often think of angels as being visible throughout the Bible. Angels were at work at all times, but visible appearances were reserved for times of special crisis or revelation. This was the most special of all times, for this angel came to announce the birth of the Lord Jesus. The earlier appearances had been to individuals (Zechariah, Mary, and Joseph). This is the first appearance of an angel to announce the birth to a group. This is also the first announcement of the birth to any person or group beyond the inner circle of the family of Jesus.

In the phrase **the glory of the Lord shone round about them,** the word **glory** is *doxa,* the New Testament fulfillment of the Old Testament glory of the Lord. This was the manifestation of the presence of the Lord among His people. The appearance of this shining glory set the stage for two sets of three things foretold by the angel.

Verse 10 contains three important truths. For one thing, the angel brought **good tidings.** This is the Greek verb *euangelizomai,* which means "to proclaim good news." This word was a favorite of Luke's. It is found 55 times in the New Testament. Of these 10 are in Luke and 15 are in Acts. This was an ordinary Greek word used in everyday speech to tell all kinds of good news. The Bible uses the word to tell the good news of salvation in Jesus Christ. Jesus used the word when He described His mission (4:18).

The second thing of significance in verse 10 is that the good news would be **of great joy. Great joy** replaced great fear. This joy is a theme of Luke's Gospel (1:14; 2:10; 10:17; 24:41,52). It is also in the Book of Acts. For example, after Philip preached Christ in the city of Samaria, "there was great joy in that city" (Acts 8:8). Joy is a key fruit of the Spirit (Gal. 5:22).

The third feature of verse 10 is that the good news of great joy was **to all people.** That the shepherds were the first to hear the message of Christ's birth illustrates that the good news was for all levels of society. Jesus exemplified this in His ministry by going to outcasts such as the tax collectors and sinners whom the Pharisees excluded. The Book of Acts shows how the good news broke through barriers of race and tradition to be told to all kinds of people. We cannot really claim to be followers of the Christ of the Gospels unless we are committed to sharing the good news of great joy with all people. Surely the Christmas season provides unique opportunities for doing this. This includes not only supporting international missions by going, giving, and praying; it also includes reaching out in our communities and sharing Christ with family and friends.

Verses 11-12: **For unto you is born this day in the city of David a Savior, which is Christ the Lord.** **¹²And this shall be a sign unto you; Ye shall find the babe wrapped in swaddling clothes, lying in a manger.**

Verse 11 announced to the shepherds **unto you is born this day.** On that very day this special birth had taken place. Verse 11 contains three important titles for the newborn baby: **Savior . . . Christ . . . Lord.**

Savior describes Jesus in terms of His mission. The angel had told Joseph to name the virgin-born Son of God "Jesus" because He would save His people from their sins (Matt. 1:21). The name Jesus means "the Lord saves." The angel made clear that He came to save people from sin. **Savior** was a popular title in ancient times. It often was used of earthly rulers to describe their deliverance of the people from those things that threatened them. Of all the things that threaten humanity, sin and its ally death are the greatest and most dangerous. Jesus came to give Himself in order to save people from sin and death.

Christ is the Greek equivalent of the Hebrew word from which we get *Messiah.* Both words mean "anointed one." In ancient times, especially in Israel, kings were anointed with oil to signify their ascension to the throne. God had promised David that one of his descendants would reign over an eternal kingdom. This promised One came to be called "the Messiah." The angel was telling these Jewish shepherds that the One born that day was this promised Messiah. Many first-century Jews wanted an earthly king, but Jesus came to be not only the Messiah but also the Suffering Servant who would fulfill His mission through death and resurrection.

Lord translates *kurios.* This word was used by the Jews to refer to God. This was also another of the titles often ascribed to earthly kings such as Caesar Augustus. Jesus was fully human, but He was also fully divine. Divinity often was ascribed to the Caesars, but only Jesus is truly divine. While the reign of Augustus was long and fruitful, it was nothing compared to the everlasting kingdom of the Son of God.

What was the **sign** of which the angel spoke? One meaning is that it was a means of identifying the baby Jesus. There was that day only one **babe wrapped in swaddling clothes, lying in a manger.** Other babies may have been born in Bethlehem on that day. Some of them may have been wrapped in those kind of clothes. But only one was laid in an animal's feeding trough for His bed. This would help the shepherds to recognize in the humble circumstances of Jesus' birth that He came to save people such as they were.

What are the lasting lessons of verses 8-12?

1. The coming of Jesus Christ into the world is the good news.
2. He came to provide the opportunity for salvation to all people.
3. He fulfilled the hope for the Messiah-King.
4. He is the divine-human Lord.

Praise the God of Grace (Luke 2:13-14)

*Who were the **heavenly host**? What is the meaning of their twofold words of praise?*

Verses 13-14: **And suddenly there was with the angel a multitude of the heavenly host praising God, and saying, [14]Glory to God in the highest, and on earth peace, good will toward men.**

A careful wording of the Greek translated **a multitude of the heavenly host** indicates "the whole host of heaven was praising God, not merely that portion of it which was visible to the shepherds."[3] Heaven indeed was filled with His praises, and the shepherds were privileged to hear this.

The heavenly hosts' praises were focused on two things: One was in heaven and the other was on earth. **The highest** often refers to God, but here it refers to heaven. The heavens were resounding with praises of **Glory to God. On earth** the birth of Jesus meant **peace, good will toward men.** For the phrase **good will toward men,** some of the Greek manuscripts have *en anthropois eudokia;* other ancient manuscripts have *en anthropois eudokias.* The one letter of difference indicates the difference between the nominative and the genitive cases. Most translations follow the genitive case and read "to men on whom his favor rests" or something similar (NIV, NRSV, NASB, NEB, REB, HCSB). The *King James Version* follows the former reading.

The **good will** is not a quality of people but of God. It is the favor of God. This is another way of speaking of the grace of God. He pours out

His peace based on His grace for sinful humanity. This **peace** is the peace with God that only God can give, and it comes through the death of Jesus for our sins. Peace is precious to every generation, but we usually think of peace as something we can attain for ourselves and consisting of the absence of hostilities. True peace is the gift of God, and the heavenly host praised God for providing true peace through Christ. During the reign of Augustus, the world experienced a long period of peace, for which much credit was given to the emperor. Epictetus [ep-ih-TEE-tuhs] was a pagan writer of the time. He wrote these words of insight: "While the emperor may give peace from war on land and sea, he is unable to give peace from passion, grief, and envy. He cannot give peace of heart, for which man yearns more than even for outward peace."[4]

What are some of the lasting lessons of verses 13-14?

1. Believers should join the heavenly host in praising God for sending His Son as the Savior.

2. Christmas should be a time of praises.

Spread the Amazing Message (Luke 2:15-20)

What decision did the shepherds make? Why did they act right away? What did they see? What did they tell others? How did this affect the others? In what sense did Mary keep these things in her heart? What did the shepherds do as they returned to their flocks? What three special privileges did the shepherds have?

Verses 15-20: And it came to pass, as the angels were gone away from them into heaven, the shepherds said one to another, Let us now go even unto Bethlehem, and see this thing which is come to pass, which the Lord hath made known unto us. [16]And they came with haste, and found Mary, and Joseph, and the babe lying in a manger. [17]And when they had seen it, they made known abroad the saying which was told them concerning this child. [18]And all they that heard it wondered at those things which were told them by the shepherds. [19]But Mary kept all these things, and pondered them in her heart. [20]And the shepherds returned, glorifying and praising God for all the things that they had heard and seen, as it was told unto them.

The shepherds had three special privileges: (1) They were the first outsiders to hear of the Savior's birth. (2) They were the first to see Jesus. (3) They were the first humans to tell the amazing message.

When **the angels were gone away from them into heaven,** the shepherds discussed what they would do about what they had heard. With the glow of the angels gone, some might have argued that they were just seeing things. But they decided to do what the angel had told them. Thus their decision was, **Let us now go even unto Bethlehem, and see this thing which is come to pass, which the Lord hath made known unto us.** They obviously believed that the angel spoke for the Lord. They probably did not spend a long time making this decision, because **they came with haste.** They lost no time in taking advantage of this unique opportunity.

The shepherds found just what the angel had told them. They **found Mary, and Joseph, and the babe lying in a manger.** The shepherds were the only ones mentioned in the Bible as coming to see Jesus on the day of His birth. The wise men came later (see Matt. 2:11). Only the humble shepherds were there—at God's invitation.

When the shepherds left, **they made known abroad the saying which was told them concerning this child.** This means they told people that the Child was the Savior, Christ, the Lord. They were the first people to have the opportunity to proclaim the amazing message, and they took full advantage of this opportunity.

And what was the response of those who heard the shepherds' message? **All they that heard it wondered** ("were amazed," NIV, HCSB) **at those things which were told them by the shepherds.** Apparently the shepherds were considered respectable enough for the people of Bethlehem to listen to their strange message.

We are not told what happened to these first hearers of these witnesses. But we are told of Mary's response to the events of the birth of Jesus. She **kept all these things, and pondered them in her heart.** She must have often recalled the events of that first day in the life of Jesus, especially when she stood at the foot of the cross years later.

As for the shepherds, they **returned** to their flocks; however, they returned different people from what they had been before the angel had come. They were **glorifying and praising God for all the things that they had heard and seen.** These things "were just as they had been told" (NIV).

What are the lasting lessons in verses 15-20?

1. We should hasten to go to Jesus.
2. God's promises are true.
3. We should tell others what we have seen and heard about Jesus.
4. Christmas is a special time for praising and glorifying God.

❖ *Spiritual Transformations*

An angel told a group of shepherds of the birth of the Savior, Christ, the Lord. A heavenly host declared God's glory in heaven and His grace on earth. The shepherds went to see Jesus and told others what the Lord had made known to them.

The three main points of this lesson are crucial aspects of a Christian celebration of Christmas. We always should be open to hear the good news of salvation in Christ. We should praise the Lord for sending the Savior. We should tell others the amazing message about Jesus. How well do you do in each of these three areas?

Have you heard and responded positively to the good news? _____

_____

Are you praising the Lord in worship and in lifestyle? _____

_____

Are you telling others the amazing message? _____

_____

Prayer of Commitment: Lord, help me to trust Christ as my Savior, to praise You by word and deed, and to tell others the amazing message of Your grace. Amen.

[1]Henry Law, in *The Book of Jesus,* ed. by Calvin Miller [Nashville: Broadman & Holman Publishers, 1996, 1998], 55.

[2]Hobbs, *An Exposition of the Gospel of Luke,* 51.

[3]Alfred Plummer, *A Critical and Exegetical Commentary on the Gospel According to Luke,* 4th ed., in The International Critical Commentary [Edinburgh: T. & T. Clark, 1905], 57.

[4]Quoted in Geldenhuys, *The Gospel of Luke,* 112.

LEADING TO WORSHIP

Bible Passage: Matthew 2:1-12
Key Verse: Matthew 2:11

❖ *Significance of the Lesson*

• The *Theme* of this lesson is that God led the wise men to Jesus so they could worship Him.

• The *Life Question* this lesson seeks to address is, What is the right way to worship?

• The *Biblical Truth* is that as the Savior and Ruler of God's people, Jesus is worthy of our worship and reverent devotion.

• The *Life Impact* is to help you worship and be devoted to Jesus the Savior.

Different Views of Worship

The prevailing secular mind-set knows little about worship and devotion to Jesus as Savior and Lord. Some secular people oppose worship. Many ignore worship. Others only go through the motions. Affiliation with a religious group or institution is viewed merely as one way of making friends and potential business contacts.

In the biblical worldview, worship is a basic human need. God sent His Son to be our Savior and Lord. As such He is worthy of genuine and consistent worship and devotion. Worship should be joyful, eager, reverent, and obedient. It should be done with others and also alone with God.

Word Study: *worship, worshiped*

The Greek verb for *worship (proskuneo)* occurs three times in Matthew 2:1-12 (vv. 2,8,11). The basic meaning is "to kneel down." It can mean "to pay homage," as to a king or an important person, but when the object is God or God's Son the meaning is "worship." In Matthew 2, some translations have "pay homage" (NRSV, REB, NEB); others affirm that the wise men worshiped Jesus (NIV, NASB, HCSB).

This lesson assumes the wise men worshiped Jesus. The word is clearly used of worshiping Jesus in Matthew 14:33 and 28:9,17.

❖ *Search the Scriptures*

The wise men saw the star and came to Jerusalem to find the King of the Jews to worship him. Herod was disturbed at this possible rival to his throne and schemed to find Him. He found out the town where the Scriptures said the Messiah would be born. He found out when the wise men had seen the star. Then he asked them to report to him when they had found the child. The wise men rejoiced as they followed the star to where the child was. They offered Him precious gifts as they worshiped Him. God warned them not to return to Herod, and they went home without seeing the king.

The three points in the Focal Passage Outline are steps in achieving the Life Impact of worshiping and being devoted to Jesus the Savior.

Worship the One Who Is Worthy (Matt. 2:1-2)

When and where was Jesus born? Who were the wise men? How did they know to come seeking the King of the Jews? What was the long-range significance of their coming to worship Jesus? Why is Jesus worthy of worship?

Verses 1-2: Now when Jesus was born in Bethlehem of Judea in the days of Herod the king, behold, there came wise men from the east to Jerusalem, ²saying, Where is he that is born King of the Jews? for we have seen his star in the east, and are come to worship him.

These verses summarize *who, when, where,* and *what* of the passage. The personalities were Jesus, the wise men, and Herod. The human focus is on the **wise men** ("Magi," NIV), but Jesus is the main person even though He was a small child at the time. The wise men, who did not yet know Jesus, were seeking the **King of the Jews.**

Who were the wise men? Tradition calls them kings. Some traditions even give them the names of Melchior, Caspar, and Belthasar. The idea that they were kings probably came from Psalm 72:10-11. Actually, they were a combination of priests and astrologers/astronomers. In the East they were from a class highly regarded by kings as counselors and predictors of future events. They came **from the east,** probably from Persia or Babylonia.

The wise men came **when Jesus was born . . . in the days of Herod the king.** The first part of this reads literally, "now Jesus having been born." In other words, the wise men did not arrive on the night of His birth (see v. 11). To indicate this many translations use the word "after" instead of **when** (NASB, NIV, NRSV, HCSB).

The wise men came to **Jerusalem,** probably because that was where the star led them. The star then seems to have become stationary or invisible to them (v. 9). So they went to the ruling king of the Jews, Herod, and asked, **Where is he that is born King of the Jews? for we have seen his star in the east, and are come to worship him.** We assume that the star appeared when Jesus was born. Herod later asked them when they had first seen the star. Presumably they told him no more than two years earlier, since when Herod killed the boy babies of Bethlehem, those two years old was the limit. Since Herod died in 4 B.C., Jesus was born sometime between 7 and 5 B.C.

How did the wise men know about the birth of the King of the Jews? They had **seen his star in the east. In the east** doesn't mean that they looked from the west to the east, but they were in the East when they saw the star. The wise men were a combination of astrologers and astronomers. They studied the stars to note their movements, but they also believed that the stars delivered messages to earthbound people. The Greek word for **star** is *astera,* from which we get the words *astronomy* and *astrology.* Stars have a mixed role in the Bible. On the one hand, they are part of God's good creation that reveals His handiwork (Ps. 19:1; Isa. 40:26). Yet stars were also worshiped and were (and still are) used in astrological predictions. Astronomy is a valid branch of science, but astrology is condemned in the Bible as pagan superstition (Isa. 47:13). Yet ironically a star was used by God to communicate to the wise men. Thus Matthew saw this revelation in a star in a positive way. Perhaps Matthew was influenced by Numbers 24:17, "A star will come out of Jacob; a scepter will arise out of Israel" (NIV).

There is much about this star that we don't know. Many people have tried to identify this star with some known heavenly phenomenon, but the best explanation is that the star was a divine creation for this special purpose. Whatever it was, the wise men saw it as **his star.** They came to worship the **King of the Jews.** Perhaps the wise men were familiar with Jewish Scriptures, since many Jews lived in those eastern countries. In some way, God revealed enough to these men that they made the long journey to find the child so they could worship Him.

Those years were times of deep yearning for better times. Many felt that the hope would be fulfilled in events in the land of the Jews. This feeling was not just in Judea but also throughout the world. This yearning is seen in the writings of the day. "Referring back to this time Suetonius in his *Life of Vespasian* says, 'There had spread all over the Orient an old established belief, that it was fated at that time for men coming from Judea to rule the world.' The same thought is found in the *Histories* of Tacitus. Josephus mentions it in his *Wars of the Jews*. At about the time of Jesus' birth the Roman poet, Virgil, wrote of the golden age that was to come."[1] The wise men probably shared in this hope for a better age. We don't know how much they understood about this King of the Jews, but they knew enough to set out to seek Him.

> Sages, leave your contemplations,
> Brighter visions beam afar;
> Seek the great Desire of nations,
> Ye have seen the Infant's star:
> Come and worship, come and worship,
> Worship Christ, the newborn King![2]

The coming of the wise men had deep, long-range significance. They were the first Gentiles to seek and worship the new King. Thus they were the first in a vast harvest of Gentiles to worship Jesus. They were from the upper class of well-educated people of their land. Thus they complement the worship of the lowly Jewish shepherds who were the first to see the newborn King. Thus both poor Jewish shepherds and educated pagan Gentiles came to worship Jesus.

What are the lasting lessons in verses 1-2?

1. People in every generation have a yearning that can only be met through a right relationship with God in Jesus Christ.

2. As King, Savior, and incarnate Son of God, Jesus is worthy of worship.

3. Those who truly want to worship Jesus will go to great lengths to do so. This speaks to us in a land of many churches in which people can worship and are free to worship God according to our own convictions. Yet many people—some of them church members—do not worship the Lord. Such people are put to shame by the example of the wise men and by the example of people in lands of few churches and in which worship is forbidden. Many make great sacrifices and take great risks to come and worship the Lord.

4. All people and all people groups need the salvation Jesus offers.

Avoid Pretense (Matt. 2:3-8)

Why did the coming of the wise men trouble Herod and all Jerusalem? How did Herod find out where the Messiah was to be born? What response did the scribes and chief priests make? How did Herod try to find out when the new King was born? How did he try to find out where He was living? Why did the wise men not see through Herod's deceit?

Verse 3: When Herod the king had heard these things, he was troubled, and all Jerusalem with him.

The word used to describe how Herod felt when he **had heard these things** is *etarachthe.* It means **troubled** ("frightened," NRSV; "deeply disturbed," HCSB; "greatly perturbed," NEB, REB). Anyone familiar with the story of Herod's reign will understand why the innocent question of the wise men terrified Herod. The same history explains why the whole city of **Jerusalem** also was disturbed. Herod had been king of the Jews for 33 years. During his ruthless reign, he was constantly on guard against anyone taking his power from him. He became so paranoid that he killed anyone even suspected of having part in a plot against him. He had some of his own sons executed. His ruthlessness was known far and wide. Caesar Augustus quipped that he had rather be Herod's pig than his son. This was a play on words since the Greek word for *son* is *huios* and the word for *pig* is *hus.* The people of Jerusalem feared another blood bath growing out of Herod's fears.

Herod feared someone else taking over his universe over which he had ruled. He need not have feared Jesus because Jesus did not aspire to be a political ruler. In fact, Jesus came to save sinners. If Herod had accepted this before he went out into eternity, he could have been saved.

> Why art thou troubled, Herod? what vain fear
> Thy blood-revolving breast to rage doth move?
> Heaven's King, who doffs himself weak flesh to wear,
> Comes not to rule in wrath, but serve in love;
> Nor would he this thy feared crown from thee tear,
> But give thee a better with himself above.
> Poor jealousy! why should he wish to prey
> Upon thy crown, who gives his own away?[3]

Verses 4-6: And when he had gathered all the chief priests and scribes of the people together, he demanded of them where Christ should be born. [5]And they said unto him, In Bethlehem of Judea:

for thus it is written by the prophet, **⁶And thou Bethlehem, in the land of Judah, art not the least among the princes of Judah: for out of thee shall come a Governor, that shall rule my people Israel.**

Herod called a meeting of **all the chief priests and scribes of the people.** He asked them **where Christ** ("the Messiah," NASB, NRSV, HCSB) **should be born.** The use of the title **Christ** for the **King of the Jews** shows that Herod and the Jewish religious leaders saw these two titles as referring to the same person. The religious leaders knew the Old Testament and quickly referred Herod to the familiar messianic text in Micah 5:2, which identifies **Bethlehem** as the Messiah's birthplace. The fact that the Messiah was to be born in Bethlehem was well known among the Jews (John 7:42). Bethlehem was the home of David, and thus the Son of David was also born there.

Matthew interpreted the Old Testament text in light of the fact that the Messiah already had been born. In Micah's day the town was little and of no importance, but now the place was **not the least among the princes of Judah.** The prophet referred to the Messiah as **a Governor** ("ruler," NIV) who would **rule** or shepherd God's people Israel. The last part of verse 6 is from 2 Samuel 5:2, where David was called the shepherd of Israel and identified as the one who would rule God's people.

What did the chief priests and scribes do with their knowledge of the birthplace of the Messiah? They knew that the wise men had come seeking One born King of the Jews, but they did not go to Bethlehem to seek Him. They are typical of those who know about Christ and the need to worship Him, but they do nothing with this knowledge.

***Verses 7-8:* Then Herod, when he had privily called the wise men, inquired of them diligently what time the star appeared. ⁸And he sent them to Bethlehem, and said, Go and search diligently for the young child; and when ye have found him, bring me word again, that I may come and worship him also.**

Herod had found out *where* Jesus was born. Now he was trying to find out *when* He was born. The word translated **privily** is the same word as in 1:19. It can mean "secretly" (NASB, REB, NRSV, NIV, HCSB) or "in private" (NEB). Herod held a secret or private meeting with the wise men, in which he **inquired of them diligently what time** ("the exact time," NIV) **the star appeared.** Herod assumed the star appeared at the time of Jesus' birth. The wily king pretended he was interested in seeking the child to **worship him.** The information the wise men gave Herod enabled him to know the child's approximate age. We do not know exactly what they told him, but we do know that Herod later ordered the slaughter of all boy babies in Bethlehem who were two years old and younger. This is crucial data in seeking to determine the year of Jesus' birth.

Why did the wise men not see through Herod's pretense? They apparently did not know his murderous reputation. They were honest, trusting men; they assumed Herod was the same kind of person. If he said he wanted to worship the new King, they believed him. Of course, Herod had a long history of lies and deceit; therefore, he found it easy to trick these foreigners. He no doubt spoke the words of verse 8 with apparent sincerity. However, we know he was lying. He is an example of people who violently oppose the cause of Christ, and he is also an example of the kind of pretense to avoid in worship.

Some people are conscious of their hypocrisy, as Herod was of his. Their sins are blatant; any claims they make that they want to worship are false. Other people may not be as conscious of their own pretense. They assume that going through the motions of worship constitutes worship. It does not. The sincerity of the wise men stands in stark contrast to the evil motives of Herod.

What are the lasting lessons of verses 3-8?

1. Some people know what the Bible says, but they fail to worship Jesus.

2. Some people are enemies of Christ who want to destroy Him and His way.

3. Pretense in worship is hypocritical worship.

Show Reverent Devotion (Matt. 2:9-12)

What do we know about the movements of the star? How is the joy of the wise men described? Which traditions about the wise men are not based on the Bible? Where did the wise men find Jesus? How did they show their reverence for Jesus? What is the significance of their gifts? What quality of theirs is seen in verse 12?

Verses 9-10: When they had heard the king, they departed; and, lo, the star, which they saw in the east, went before them, till it came and stood over where the young child was. [10]When they saw the star, they rejoiced with exceeding great joy.

Many mysteries remain about the star and its movements. Did it first appear on the day of the birth of the King of the Jews? Did it move or stand still? Did it first lead the wise men to Jerusalem? Did it disappear or remain over Jerusalem? Craig Blomberg observed about verse 9: "This is the first time the star is actually said to move. The text leaves open the question of whether or not it had moved previously. If it had not, this would explain why the Magi had managed to get only as far as Jerusalem. They may have seen the star above Israel and assumed that its ruler would be born in the capital. But regardless of how much the star had traveled, its motion here seems to require a supernatural event."[4] What we do know is that **the star . . . went before them, till it came and stood over where the young child was.**

The fact that **when they saw the star, they rejoiced with exceeding great joy** implies that the star had not been visible since they reached Jerusalem. Verse 10 has in common with Luke 2:10 the words **great joy.** However, Matthew 2:10 uses not only the noun for **joy** but also the verb form from the same root—**rejoiced.** The *New International Version* combines the two words into "overjoyed." The *New Revised Standard Version* has "overwhelmed with joy." The *Holman Christian Standard Bible* has "overjoyed beyond measure." This kind of joy ought to be part of our worship experiences: "Make a joyful noise unto the LORD, all ye lands. Serve the LORD with gladness: come into his presence with singing" (Ps. 100:1-2).

Verses 11-12: **And when they were come into the house, they saw the young child with Mary his mother, and fell down, and worshiped him: and when they had opened their treasures, they presented unto him gifts; gold, and frankincense, and myrrh.** [12]**And being warned of God in a dream that they should not return to Herod, they departed into their own country another way.**

Many popular legends have developed about the wise men and their part in the coming of Christ. These often are seen in pageants, nativity scenes, cards, and songs. The most serious of these is the picture of the wise men with the shepherds worshiping Jesus on the night of His birth in Bethlehem. Matthew 2:11 describes the wise men's first meeting with Jesus. Jesus is described as a **young child.** This translates *paidion,* a different word from that used for a newborn infant (compare "babe," *brephos,* in Luke 2:16). Jesus was still in Bethlehem when the wise men visited, but He was in a **house.** This was not the temporary shelter found by Joseph on the night of Jesus' birth.

Another part of the legend is that there were three wise men. This is more likely, for there were three gifts. However, the Bible never gives the number of the wise men. Before presenting their gifts, they **fell down, and worshiped him.** As we saw in the Word Study, the word for **worshiped** can mean either "to show homage" to someone great or "to worship" someone divine. The literal meaning is to "bow the knee." These wise men seem to have seen in Jesus more than a great king. Why had they come so far if He was just another human king of the Jews? They obviously did not have the full Christian revelation of Jesus Christ, but they responded with reverence to the One whom they believed to be more than human. Such reverent devotion is a crucial part of all true worship.

The wise men's joy and reverence combined in giving Him **gifts.** These are called **their treasures.** The word can refer to the treasures or to the container in which they were kept ("treasure chests," NRSV). After the wise men opened their treasure boxes, in which their gifts had been carried for many miles just for this moment, **they presented unto him gifts; gold, and frankincense, and myrrh.** These gifts "were typically associated with royalty. . . . Gold, then as now, was a precious metal prized for its beauty and value, an appropriate regal gift. Frankincense and myrrh were fragrant spices and perfumes equally appropriate for such adoration and worship."[5]

Giving worthy gifts to the Lord is still a part of how we show reverent devotion to Him. This is the season for an offering to be used to fulfill the Great Commission. What better gift to give to Jesus during the season when we celebrate His birth? Our offerings to the Lottie Moon Christmas Offering for International Missions make possible international missionary work.

Another characteristic of the wise men is reinforced by their actions in verse 12. Just as they had been sensitive to God's message when they saw and followed the star, so were they sensitive to His warning **in a dream that they should not return to Herod.** Therefore, they returned to **their own country** by a different route than they had intended. They thus did not go back to tell Herod where Jesus could be found. This quality of sensitivity and obedience to God is also a mark of true worship.

To illustrate this point, Herschel Hobbs referred to the play *St. Joan* by George Bernard Shaw. "In the coronation scene in Rheims Cathedral Joan tells of hearing the voice calling her to deliver France. But Charles, the weak king, interrupts her. 'O, your voices, your voices! Why don't the voices come to me? I am king, not you.' Joan replies, 'They do come to you; but you do not hear them. When the angelus rings you cross yourself and have done with it; but if you prayed from your heart, and listened to the trilling of the bells in the air after they stop ringing, you would hear the voices as well as I do.'"[6]

Those who are open to hear God's voice hear His voice or receive His message however He sends it. When we hear, we obey without question or delay.

What are the lasting truths of verses 9-12?

1. Those who seek to worship Christ will have opportunities to do so.
2. Joy is a mark of genuine worship.
3. Reverence and devotion are at the heart of worship.
4. Giving is part of worship.
5. Obedience is the result of a heart open to hear and do God's will.

❖ *Spiritual Transformations*

The wise men followed the star and traveled far, hoping to worship the new King of the Jews. Herod was troubled at their coming and set out to find where and when this King had been born. The wise men followed the star to where Jesus was, and they worshiped Him there.

Our English word *worship* comes from an old word for "worth." When we worship, we reveal what we consider most worthy of our devotion. What does your worship reveal about your values and what you consider most important? Evaluate your worship practices in light of the three outline points.

How much effort do you put into finding opportunities to worship the Lord? _____

Is there any element of pretense in your worship? Do you worship only in public where you can be seen? _____

How much reverent devotion is part of your worship? _____

Prayer of Commitment: Lord Jesus, You are worthy to receive all my devotion. Accept my gifts, songs, prayers, and other acts of worship. Amen.

[1] Hobbs, *An Exposition of the Gospel of Matthew*, 25.
[2] James Montgomery, "Angels, from the Realms of Glory," *The Baptist Hymnal* [Nashville: Convention Press, 1991], 94.
[3] Richard Crashaw, "Herod's Suspicions," in *The Book of Jesus*, 139.
[4] Blomberg, "Matthew," NAC, 65.
[5] Blomberg, "Matthew," NAC, 65-66.
[6] Hobbs, *An Exposition of the Gospel of Matthew*, 30.

Study Theme

Promises of Grace

Standing on the promises that cannot fail,
When the howling storms of doubt and fear assail,
By the living Word of God I shall prevail,
Standing on the promises of God.[1]

The promises of God are precious to His people. In this four-session Study Theme we will focus on four of God's promises of grace. Included are His promise of peace in the place of anxiety, His promise of deliverance from temptation, His promise of life's value, and His promise of a future place in Jesus' presence.

The first lesson, "The Promise of Peace," is a study of Matthew 6:25-34, Jesus' call to avoid anxiety and seek first God's kingdom, and of Matthew 11:28-30, Jesus' invitation for the weary to find rest in Him. The second lesson, "The Promise of Deliverance," is based on 1 Corinthians 10:6-13, where Paul warned of overconfidence and told how God provides a way to overcome temptation, and on James 1:13-15, which shows how temptation becomes sin and sin leads to death. The third lesson, "The Promise of Life's Value," is based on Psalm 139:7-16, which affirms the beginning of life within the womb, and on Mark 10:13-16, which tells how Jesus blessed little children. The is the annual *Sanctity of Human Life Lesson.* The fourth lesson, "The Promise of Heaven," is based on John 14:1-4, in which Jesus promised to come again and take His followers to a place prepared for them, and on Revelation 21:1-5 and 22:1-5, which describe the new heaven and new earth.

The promises of grace are given by God, but claiming each promise calls for appropriate responses by you. Each promise has a practical application.

This study is designed to help you—
• stop worrying (Jan. 5)
• resist temptation (Jan. 12)
• value and protect human life (Jan. 19)
• live each day in anticipation of heaven (Jan. 26)

[1]R. Kelso Carter, "Standing on the Promises," No. 335, *The Baptist Hymnal*, 1991.

THE PROMISE OF PEACE

Bible Passage: Matthew 6:25-34; 11:28-30
Key Verse: Matthew 6:33

❖ *Significance of the Lesson*

• The *Theme* of this lesson is that God's promise of grace includes peace in place of worry.

• The *Life Question* this lesson seeks to address is, Why should I stop worrying?

• The *Biblical Truth* is that because of God's promise to provide, believers do not have to be overcome by worry.

• The *Life Impact* is to help you stop worrying.

Worry and Anxiety

Stress is part of life. People live under constant pressures of all kinds. Those who leave God out of their lives are left to cope with these pressures on their own. Factors such as the breakdown of social structures and economic uncertainties make people subject to worry. Worry shows itself physically, mentally, socially, and spiritually in a multitude of ways.

In the biblical worldview, worry is often the result of misplaced priorities. Believers have no need to worry about the necessities of life because God has promised to provide all we need to do His will. Adults can choose between worry and trust in God.

Word Study: *take thought, taking thought*

Take thought and **taking thought** in Matthew 6 translate the Greek verb *merimnao*. This word comes from *merizo*, which means "to divide," and *meris*, which means "a part." When combined into one word, the idea is something like our phrase "coming apart at the seams." The word means "worry" (NIV, HCSB, NKJV, NRSV, CEV) or "anxious" (NEB, REB). Anxiety or worry distract and divide a person's energies and commitments. **Take thought** meant the same thing in 1611 when the

King James Version was translated as we mean today by *worry*. Today, the negative words **take no thought** seem to imply that we are to give no thought to these things. Jesus was not condemning planning or giving forethought to things. He was condemning letting them distract us from more important things. Obviously this is the key word in Matthew 6:25-34. It is found in verses 25,27,28,31, and twice in verse 34.

❖ *Search the Scriptures*

Jesus taught His followers not to worry about meeting their physical needs, for worry never accomplishes any good. He pointed out that worry is a mark of unbelievers and should not be for those who trust God as Father. He called them to seek first the concerns of God, and He would care for their concerns. Jesus called those with burdens to come to Him for rest and purpose.

The Focal Passage Outline points provide reasons to stop worrying.

Worry Is Unproductive (Matt. 6:25-27)

*How do these verses relate to the preceding verses? What point did Jesus make by mentioning **the fowls of the air**? What did Jesus say about **life**? Does verse 27 refer to growth in height or to a span of time?*

6:25-27: Therefore I say unto you, Take no thought for your life, what ye shall eat, or what ye shall drink; nor yet for your body, what ye shall put on. Is not the life more than meat, and the body than raiment? 26Behold the fowls of the air: for they sow not, neither do they reap, nor gather into barns; yet your heavenly Father feedeth them. Are ye not much better than they? 27Which of you by taking thought can add one cubit unto his stature?

The word **therefore** ties verses 25-34 to verses 19-24. This entire part of the Sermon on the Mount deals with the proper attitude toward material things. Jesus challenged His disciples to focus on heavenly treasures rather than earthly treasures (vv. 19-21), to see life's realities through the focused vision of single-minded devotion to God (vv. 22-23), and to give their total obedience to God rather than to things (v. 24). In verses 25-34 He warned them of the subtle dangers of worldly anxiety. Even people of faith are tempted to worry. Believers need to defeat worry through trust in God and through total commitment to His kingdom and righteousness.

The form of the verb in verse 25 refers to continuous action and can mean "don't keep on worrying" or even "stop worrying." **Life** is the word *psyche,* which is used here to refer to our lives as creations of God. The problem with worry is that it forgets what life is really all about. Among the needs for sustaining our lives are food and clothing, but we should not be paralyzed with fears and worries about what we will **eat,** what we will **drink,** and what we will **put on** ("wear," NIV). Jesus asked, "Is not life more important than food, and the body more important than clothes?" (NIV). On another occasion, He said, "A man's life does not consist in the abundance of his possessions" (Luke 12:15, NIV).

Jesus called His hearers' attention to the birds. They do none of the things that people do to provide food: **sow** or **reap** or store in **barns.** Yet, Jesus declared, **your heavenly Father feedeth them.** Jesus then argued from the lesser to the greater. He asked, "Are you not much more valuable than they?"(NIV). The fact that God feeds the birds shows He cares for them. God takes note of the fall of the smallest sparrow. Yet humans are made in God's image, capable of eternal fellowship with God. If God cares for the birds, how much more will He care for us?

Some critics have accused Jesus of promoting laziness because of His comments on not worrying about basic needs. But they miss the point. Birds are not creatures that wait for God to feed them. They constantly forage for food. God feeds the birds, but He does it by providing a world filled with food and the means for them to feed themselves. Thus Jesus was not saying that people should fold their hands and wait for God to feed them. The birds are examples not of idleness but of the absence of anxiety. People of faith still must sow, reap, and store their food; but there is no contradiction between working and praying, "Give us this day our daily bread" (v. 11). As Christians, we should do their part in providing for the physical necessities of life, but we should place our trust in God to provide what we need, not constantly worry about these things as if only our efforts can provide them.

Said the Robin to the Sparrow:
    "I should really like to know
Why these anxious human beings
    Rush about and worry so."
Said the Sparrow to the Robin:
    "Friend, I think that it must be
That they have no heavenly Father
    Such as cares for you and me."[1]

Some translations of verse 27 assume Jesus was talking about an increase in height, and others think He was referring to a span of time. The *King James Version* has, **Which of you by taking thought** ("worrying," NKJV) **can add one cubit unto his stature? Statue** translates *helikian*. This word is used as a measure of height in Luke 19:3, where Zacchaeus was called "little of stature." **Cubit** translates *pechun*, which originally meant "forearm" but came to mean a unit for measuring distance. Thus Jesus may have been speaking of adding to one's height about 18 inches. The *New King James Version*, the *New English Bible*, and the *Holman Christian Standard Bible* also accept this view. But *helikian* can also refer to a span of time. Therefore, some translations have, "Who of you by worrying can add a single hour to his life?" (NIV; see also NRSV, NASB, CEV, REB). Herschel Hobbs wrote: "'Stature' is used in the papyri for both height and length of life. Either makes sense here. However, in view of the context ('life') the latter seems more appropriate. Anxiety certainly does not lengthen one's life. Indeed, it more likely will shorten it."[2] Thus worry is not only unproductive but also dangerous to one's life and health. Many physical and emotional problems grow out of continual worrying.

What are the lasting lessons from verses 25-27?

1. Believers should not worry about the material necessities of life.

2. We should do our part to provide these necessities but place our ultimate trust in God's provision.

3. Worry not only does not add time to our lives but can harm health and shorten life.

Worry Is Unbelief (Matt. 6:28-32)

*What lesson did Jesus teach using **the lilies of the field**? Why is worry a sign of **little faith**? In what sense **do the Gentiles seek** these things?*

6:28-32: And why take ye thought for raiment? Consider the lilies of the field, how they grow; they toil not, neither do they spin: [29]And yet I say unto you, That even Solomon in all his glory was not arrayed like one of these. [30]Wherefore, if God so clothe the grass of the field, which today is, and tomorrow is cast into the oven, shall he not much more clothe you, O ye of little faith? [31]Therefore take no thought, saying, What shall we eat? or, What shall we drink? or, Wherewithal shall we be clothed? [32](For after all these things do the Gentiles seek:) for your heavenly Father knoweth that ye have need of all these things.

In dealing with anxiety about clothes, Jesus used flowers to teach a lesson about trust in God. **The lilies of the field** probably refers to wild flowers, not to any one species. Even as birds do not sow or reap, flowers do not do what humans do to clothe themselves. The word **toil** refers to heavy work in the fields, and the term **spin** refers to the finer work done at home to make clothes.

Jesus did not present the flowers as examples of idleness any more than He did the birds. Both are examples of God's provisions for living things that are void of anxiety. Verse 29 stresses the flowers' splendor and beauty by comparing them with Solomon's proverbial splendor. His wardrobe must have been fabulous; yet when he was compared with these flowers, **even Solomon in all his glory was not arrayed like one of these.**

Verses 28-30 are another example of arguing from the lesser to the greater. Verse 30 emphasizes that **the grass of the field** has a short time to flourish. It is here one day and gone the next. **Into the oven** refers to its withering under the heat of the sun. Jesus said that if God gave such beauty to plants with a short life span, **shall he not much more clothe you, O ye of little faith?**

Little faith does not mean that His hearers had no faith. Jesus knew His followers were pilgrims of faith—on their way but not yet there. He knew the world often tempts even the most committed disciples into the subtle snare of worldly anxiety. These disciples constantly needed to seek divine strength to overcome worry and to renew their basic trust in the Heavenly Father's goodness and trustworthiness.

Jesus warned of an obsession with questions such as those in verse 31. The unbelieving people of the world are constantly concerned with things such as food, drink, and clothes. People who live on the edge of survival worry about such things. This was the kind of society in which Jesus lived. Many in our day still are struggling to survive, but many—especially in America—have grown up in an affluent society. Our concerns and worries, therefore, are for such things as prosperity, pleasure, popularity, prestige, and power. People who are rich by the standards of the rest of the world worry and fret about how to become wealthier. Those who have power are anxious that they might lose what they have or that they may not be able to get more of it. This kind of obsessive worry about secular things is a mark of those who do not know God.

Specific worries are as different as people are, and worries change as circumstances change; but all worries have some things in common. All are based on fears of an unknown future. All tend to forget that we can trust God to lead us into an unknown future and to supply whatever we need to do His will. Adults worry about getting a job, doing well at the job, and holding the job. They worry about making friends, getting married, and having children. They worry about their children's health, safety, and education. They worry about the problems their offspring face or will face. They worry about having enough money to buy what they need now and in an uncertain future. As adults age, they worry about being able to retire. After they retire, they worry about inflation and about depression. They worry about their health and the health of their families. They worry about crime and about becoming victims of crime. They worry about being alone and being dependent on others for their care.

Being concerned about these things is normal and natural. Making plans to deal with some of them is part of being a responsible person. But becoming obsessed with even these kinds of worries is a contradiction to the faith we profess. Any time we forget to trust God and to entrust our future welfare to Him, we are in danger of living like unbelievers. Failure to trust God is thus the main cause of worry. This occurs because we forget Jesus' words: **Your heavenly Father knoweth that ye have need of all these things.** And because He knows and cares, we can trust Him to provide what we need.

What are the lasting lessons from verses 28-32?

1. What people worry about varies, but most worries are based on fears of an uncertain future.

2. Obsessive worry is the opposite of faith in God.

3. We can cast all our cares on God, who knows our needs and cares for us.

Worry Is Unnecessary (Matt. 6:33-34)

*What is **the kingdom of God** and **his righteousness**? What does it mean to **seek first**? What are **all these things**? How are they **added unto** us? What is meant by **the morrow shall take thought for the things of itself**? What is meant by **sufficient unto the day is the evil thereof**?*

6:33: But seek ye first the kingdom of God, and his righteousness; and all these things shall be added unto you.

Verse 33 is the key verse in Matthew 6:25-34 and probably in the entire Sermon on the Mount. It has become for many people a key verse by which to live day by day. Verse 33 is the positive counterpart to the warnings about worry in verses 25,28,31, and 34. It is also the opposite way of life to that of the unbelievers described in verse 32. They seek material things for themselves and rely on themselves. Jesus called His followers to **seek . . . first the kingdom of God, and his righteousness.** These words refer to the fulfillment of God's purpose of redemption. God is at work to provide salvation and life for sinful humanity. He has promised that His purpose will be fulfilled.

Rather than seeking the material things sought by unbelievers, we are to **seek . . . first** the things of God. John R. W. Stott wrote: "Christ's language of search (contrasting what *the Gentiles seek* with what his followers are to *seek first,* 32, 33) introduces us to the subject of ambition. Jesus took it for granted that all human beings are 'seekers.' It is not natural for people to drift aimlessly through life like plankton. We need something to live for, something to give meaning to our existence, something to 'seek,' something on which to set our 'hearts' our and 'minds.' . . . Ambition concerns our goals in life and our incentives for pursuing them."[3] Stott went on to point out that Jesus simplified the choices for us by reducing the basic options to two. The ambition of unbelievers is the obsessive search for material things and worry about their own material security. The ambition of God's people is that God's rule and righteousness will spread and triumph.

When God's kingdom and righteous are our ambition, Jesus promised that **all these things shall be added unto you.** That is, God will supply all we need to do His will. If we focus on God and His kingdom, we can trust Him to take care of our needs. T. W. Hunt stated his own experience: "All my life I have been about the wrong business. I thought those 'things' in Matthew 6:33 were my business, and I've tried to attend to them. Now I find that God's kingdom and righteousness are *my* business and *God's* business is my things. When I released my things to God and started attending to *my* business—which is God's kingdom and righteousness—I freed God to attend to *His* business, which is my things."[4] Bruner wrote, "Jesus frees us from this world's obsession with how we're doing (how we're eating and dressing) by giving us the liberating obsession of concern with how God is doing."[5]

Jesus did not promise that we would never lack enough food or adequate clothing. He promised that we can trust God to give us what we need, not necessarily all we want.

6:34: **Take therefore no thought for the morrow: for the morrow shall take thought for the things of itself. Sufficient unto the day is the evil thereof.**

Two parts of verse 34 need to be clarified: **the morrow shall take thought for the things of itself** ("tomorrow will worry about itself," NIV; "tomorrow will bring worries of its own," NRSV) and **sufficient unto the day is the evil thereof** ("each day has enough trouble of its own," NIV; today's trouble is enough for today," NRSV).

Worries basically are fears about what may happen in an unknown future. Today is the only day in which we can live. Fears about tomorrow can leave us unprepared to face whatever tomorrow brings. Many of the things we worry about never happen, but verse 34 reminds us that sometimes they do. However, when they do, worry has made us less prepared to meet the challenges. In other words, we should live a day at a time—trusting God for His help in meeting today's challenges and relying on Him to be sufficient for us in all our unknown tomorrows.

As Abraham Lincoln traveled to Washington following his election, he was asked if civil war was coming. Lincoln told a story that was recorded by Horace Greeley. Lincoln recounted an incident from his days as a lawyer riding the circuit. He and the other lawyers had to ford several rivers. They dreaded doing this when the rivers were at flood stage. They especially feared crossing the Fox River at such a time. They spent the night in the company of a Methodist circuit rider. They asked him if he knew about crossing the Fox River. The preacher replied: "I know all about the Fox River. I have crossed it often, and understand it well. But I have one fixed rule with regard to Fox River: *I never cross it till I reach it!*"[6] Worrying about things ahead of time is an exercise in futility.

Many of our worst fears and worries never happen. Such worry is debilitating as well as useless. We can do something about some of the things we worry about. Then we ought to act rather than to worry. We cannot do something about other things. Even these ought not to foster worry; instead, we should meet them with trust in God.

What are the lasting lessons in verses 33-34?

1. We should focus on God and the coming of His kingdom rather than on our own concerns.

2. When we put God's kingdom first, He supplies all we need to do His will.

3. Each day has troubles enough of its own without adding the burden of worrying about what might happen tomorrow.

4. We should live each day trusting in God for the present and future.

Jesus Is the Source of Peace (Matt. 11:28-30)

How does this invitation compare with other Bible invitations? Who is invited? To whom are people invited? What is promised to those who respond? Is the way of Jesus hard or easy?

11:28-30: Come unto me, all ye that labor and are heavy laden, and I will give you rest. ²⁹Take my yoke upon you, and learn of me; for I am meek and lowly in heart: and ye shall find rest unto your souls. ³⁰For my yoke is easy, and my burden is light.

The Bible has some beautiful and powerful invitations. One is in Isaiah 55:1, and another is in Revelation 22:17. But none is more beautiful than this invitation of Jesus. This invitation is personal from Jesus to each person: **Come unto me.** The invitation is to go to Jesus Himself. The invitation is to **all ye that labor and are heavy laden.** Who cannot identify with this group? This invitation is for those who toil and who carry heavy burdens of any kind. We were not created strong enough to bear life's burdens alone. We need the help of God and of brothers and sisters in the faith.

Jesus promised two things: **rest** and a **yoke.** These may seem to be at cross-purposes until we look at each more carefully. He promised **rest unto your souls.** This is the same legacy of peace of which He spoke in John 14:27: "Peace I leave with you, my peace I give unto you: not as the world giveth, give I unto you. Let not your heart be troubled, neither let it be afraid."

The **yoke** was used to harness together oxen to do farm work. It also became a symbol of becoming the disciple of some teacher. This was how Jesus used it here. We are to **learn of** Jesus, or more accurately, to "learn from" (NIV) Him. He is the Teacher and the Subject of the teaching. His words are the textbook. Jesus wants us to live by what He taught. The result will be the peace that only He can give.

The hardest words to understand in the invitation are the last words: **for my yoke is easy, and my burden is light.** We recall other teachings of His, such as 7:13-14, in which He set forth the challenge and difficulty of being His follower. How can His way be both hard and easy? It is hard because Jesus calls us to live by heaven's standards in a sinful world. It is easy because He is with us and gives us joy, peace, and fulfillment when we walk with Him in His way.

Bruner offered a beautiful translation of these verses: "Come here to me all of you who are working hard and carrying too much, and I will refresh you. Here, take my yoke upon you, and learn from me, because I am gentle and simple at heart, and you will experience refreshing deep down in your lives. You see, my yoke is easy and my burden is light."[7]

What are the lasting lessons from 11:28-30?

1. Jesus personally invites us to come to Him.

2. He promises to ease our strain from toil and to help carry our heavy burdens.

3. He offers the kind of rest that comes from being properly yoked with Him and with other disciples.

❖ *Spiritual Transformations*

Jesus taught His followers not to worry because it does no good to worry. He taught that to be obsessed with worrying about things is a mark of unbelievers and that trust in God is a mark of believers. He called people to put God's concerns first, promising that God in turn would care for their concerns. He said to live one day at a time. He invited those who are heavy laden to come to Him for rest and discipleship.

Worry is a problem for most of us at some time. We need to remember that worry is unproductive, unbelieving, and unnecessary. We need to heed the invitation of Jesus to the kind of discipleship that provides true peace.

What kinds of things do you worry about? _____

What verses in this lesson can help you stop worrying if you practice them? _____

What changes in your life would be necessary to truly seek first the kingdom of God and His righteousness? _____

Prayer of Commitment: Lord Jesus, forgive me for worrying; help me to trust You more and to put the things of God first in my life. Amen.

[1]Elizabeth Cheney, "Overheard in an Orchard," in *Masterpieces of Religious Verse*, edited by James Dalton Morrison [New York: Harper & Brothers Publishers, 1948], 86.

[2]Hobbs, *An Exposition of the Gospel of Matthew*, 76.

[3]John R. W. Stott, *The Message of the Sermon on the Mount*, in The Bible Speaks Today [Downers Grove: InterVarsity Press, 1978], 160.

[4]T. W. Hunt, *The Mind of Christ* [Nashville: Broadman & Holman Publishers, 1995], 25.

[5]Bruner, *The Christbook*, 265.

[6]Carl Sandburg, *Abraham Lincoln: The Prairie Years and The War Years* [Pleasantville, New York: The Reader's Digest Association, 1970], 177.

[7]Bruner, *The Christbook*, 437.

THE PROMISE OF DELIVERANCE

Background Passage: 1 Corinthians 10:1-13; James 1:1-15
Focal Passage: 1 Corinthians 10:6-13; James 1:13-15
Key Verse: 1 Corinthians 10:13

❖ *Significance of the Lesson*

• The *Theme* of this lesson is that God's promise of grace includes deliverance from temptation.
• The *Life Question* this lesson seeks to address is, How can I resist temptation?
• The *Biblical Truth* is that God provides deliverance from temptation to those who seek His help.
• The *Life Impact* is to help you resist temptation.

Attitudes Toward Temptation

All people experience temptation. Some adults make no effort to resist because sin is their normal way of life. Others do not resist because they have so often failed to resist. Some seek to absolve themselves of any responsibility for yielding to temptation by blaming others, perhaps even God, for their wrongs. Others live in constant guilt because of their feelings of weakness.

The biblical worldview views temptations as things to be resisted, but affirms that only with God's help can temptations be overcome.

Word Study: *temptation, tempted, tempt*

The Greek verb *peirazo* can mean "to try" or "to attempt" (Acts 9:26). It more often means "to test" or "to put someone to the test." This can be in the good sense, as when God tests people of faith to strengthen their faith (Heb. 11:17). The verb also can be used in the bad sense of someone being "tempted" to do evil. This is how the verb is used in James 1:13,14. Another bad sense is when people seek to put God to the test (Matt. 16:1). The noun is *peirasmos,* which can mean "test" or "trial" in the good sense, as in James 1:2,12; or it can mean "temptation" in the bad sense, as in 1 Corinthians 10:13.

❖ *Search the Scriptures*

No one can blame God for being tempted, but each person is responsible for yielding to temptation. Christians need to be on guard against temptation rather than being overconfident. God never allows a Christian to be tempted beyond the person's ability to overcome with the Lord's help. The three outline points are ways to resist temptation.

Assume Responsibility (James 1:13-15)

Why do people often try to blame God for their sins? Why is God not responsible? At what point does temptation become sin? When are desires bad? What two terms from hunting and fishing are in the passage? What life cycle is described?

James 1:13-15: Let no man say when he is tempted, I am tempted of God: for God cannot be tempted with evil, neither tempteth he any man: [14]but every man is tempted, when he is drawn away of his own lust, and enticed. [15]Then when lust hath conceived, it bringeth forth sin: and sin, when it is finished, bringeth forth death.

James 1:1-15 shows the contrast between tests that God intends for our good and temptations that grow out of our sinful desires. Verses 1-4 show why Christians can have joy in times of trouble. God can use these trials to produce endurance. Verses 5-8 encourage prayer to receive God's wisdom to live in the right way. Verses 9-12 describe the rewards for enduring trials. Verses 13-15 move from tests that God intends to temptations that Satan seeks to use for our harm. The same experience may be intended by God for our good, but Satan and our evil desires turn it into a temptation to sin.

The words **I am tempted of** ("by," NKJV) **God** ("God is tempting me," NIV) remind us that people have a tendency to blame others for their temptations and sins. Since the time of Adam and Eve, sinners have tried to do this. When God spoke to them after their sin, Adam blamed Eve and, by implication, God Himself for giving Eve to him (Gen. 3:12). Eve blamed the tempter for his deception (v. 13).

Some people make God the direct cause for everything that happens. They overlook that God made people free and accountable for their own actions. Some form of the word *peirazo* is found four times in verse 13—**tempted** (twice) **. . . cannot be tempted . . . tempteth. Cannot be tempted** is the word *apeirasmos*—the same Greek word but with the alpha privative on the front of it, which turns the word into a negative (as in *theist* and *atheist*). The word as used here means that **God cannot be tempted with evil.** God is "untempt-able." God and evil are incompatible. Not only can God not be tempted with evil, but He does not tempt "anyone" (NIV, HCSB) to evil.

God does allow tests for our good, but He never seeks to use such tests to lead us into evil. His purpose in allowing tests is always for our good. Our sinful nature responds to the tests in such a way that we turn away from God rather then draw closer to Him. This distinction between trials for our good and temptations for our harm helps us understand the prayer Jesus taught us to pray, "Lead us not into temptation." Remember that the rest of the sentence is "deliver us from evil" (Matt. 6:13). The prayer is a confession of our weakness. We ask God to keep us from those situations in which we may be tempted, and if we find ourselves in such a situation, to enable us to overcome temptation.

James insisted that none of us can blame anyone but ourselves when we yield to temptation. A person **is tempted, when he is drawn away of his own lust, and enticed** ("each one is tempted when, by his own evil desire, he is dragged away and enticed," NIV), he wrote. **Lust** translates *epithumias,* which means "desire." The word itself is neutral; it can refer to good desires (Phil. 1:23). The context in James 1:14, however, shows that it refers to evil desires. The word was some-times used of sexual desires, but it could refer to any desire.

Why did James not mention the role of Satan in temptation? He wrote later of the devil's role and our need to submit ourselves to God and to resist the devil, promising that he will then flee from us (4:7). However, in 1:13-15 James focused on the deadly work of our own evil desires as the source of temptation. Kurt A. Richardson, writing in *The New American Commentary,* said, "We are our own cause of temp-tation, not something outside us, devil or human. This is not to say that Satan is not involved in the temptations of the world. But James was concentrating here on the role of the believer's own desires."[1]

Being tempted is not sinning. Jesus was tempted, but He did not sin (Heb. 4:15). It is not easy to identify the point at which temptation becomes sin. The task is not difficult when the temptation becomes an action; however, identifying when an inner temptation becomes sin isn't easy. When we continue to let the evil thought remain in our minds, at some point it can become sin.

The words **drawn away** and **enticed** come from the areas of fishing and hunting. A fish is lured to take the bait and is therefore caught. An animal is trapped by going after something that seems desirable. In the same way, people are snared in traps of their own making. Animals are creatures that live by instincts, but humans make their own choices for which they are accountable.

Verse 15 presents the life cycle of temptation, sin, and death. Terms from human conception, birth, growth, and death are used: **When lust hath conceived, it bringeth forth** ("gives birth to," NIV) **sin: and sin, when it is finished** ("full-grown," NIV), **bringeth forth** ("gives birth to," NIV) **death.** Flirting with temptation spawns sin; and if we continue to nurture and grow our sin to maturity, the result is death. For the unsaved, this is not only physical death but eternal death in separation from God. For believers, it may be a physical death and an existence on earth that is deathlike.

The point of verses 13-15 is clear. "The main purpose of this section is to administer a sharp rebuke to those Christians who wish to find an excuse for their sinning, in order to free themselves from personal responsibility for it."[2] The only way to avoid this deadly life cycle is to accept responsibility for our actions and to not let temptation move into sin; and when we sometimes fall into sin, to repent and find God's power to overcome.

What are the lasting lessons from James 1:13-15?

1. You have no one to blame but yourself for your sin.

2. In spite of this, many people try to blame someone else, even God.

3. God cannot be tempted, and He tempts no one.

4. God allows tests for our good, but our evil desires turn these into temptations.

5. Each of us is tempted by his or her own evil desires.

6. We are snared in traps of our own making.

7. Desire leads to temptation; if one yields, this leads to sin; if sin persists, this leads to death.

Be on Guard (1 Cor. 10:6-12)

*How does 1 Corinthians 10:1-13 fit into the larger context? In what way do Old Testament stories serve as **examples** for believers? What* *four Old Testament examples did Paul cite? How did each apply to Corinth in Paul's day? How do they apply today? Why is self-confidence a dangerous spiritual condition?*

1 Corinthians 10:6-11: Now these things were our examples, to the intent we should not lust after evil things, as they also lusted. ⁷Neither be ye idolaters, as were some of them; as it is written, The people sat down to eat and drink, and rose up to play. ⁸Neither let us commit fornication, as some of them committed, and fell in one day three and twenty thousand. ⁹Neither let us tempt Christ, as some of them also tempted, and were destroyed of serpents. ¹⁰Neither murmur ye, as some of them also murmured, and were destroyed of the destroyer. ¹¹Now all these things happened unto them for examples: and they are written for our admonition, upon whom the ends of the world are come.

The larger context of this passage—1 Corinthians 8:1–11:1—is whether to eat meat sacrificed to idols. Paul took the position in chapter 8 that since idols had no reality, eating the meat was all right. He made one exception in chapter 8 and another in chapter 10: (1) The ones who felt that it was not a moral issue ought not to eat if it caused a more scrupulous brother or sister to stumble; and (2) they should not participate in idol feasts in pagan temples.

Paul warned in 1 Corinthians 10:1-13 that privileges do not ensure that we will not fall into sin. The key to this passage's setting is in verses 14-21. Some of the Corinthians felt so confident of their moral and spiritual privileges and their strength that they felt no harm could come to them by going to a pagan feast. Many of them also seem to have felt that the rigid demands of the Christian faith did not apply to them. Paul pointed out that idols lack reality, but the evil powers used idols and idol feasts.

First Corinthians 10:1-5 shows how, in some ways, the Israelites' privileges foreshadowed those of Christians. In a sense, all were baptized in the cloud and in the Red Sea. In a sense, the manna and the water foreshadowed the Lord's Supper. Verse 6 ties together verses 1-5 with verses 6-12. Paul pointed to some incidents in the life of Israel that were **examples** for Christians.

Lust and **lusted** translate *epithumeo,* the verb form of *epithumia,* which is found in James 1:14-15. As in the case of the noun, the verb itself can refer to good or bad desires; however, Paul added the words **after evil things** to emphasize that he was writing about evil desires.

Paul warned in verse 6 that Christians ought not desire evil things the way the Israelites did. Then he gave four examples of evil things they desired and sought.

Paul warned against being **idolaters** in verse 7. Then he quoted Exodus 32:6, from the story of the golden calf. Thus Paul was writing here of that sin. While Moses was on the mountain receiving the Ten Commandments, the people pressured Aaron into making a golden calf. Exodus 32:6 describes what they did: **the people sat down to eat and drink, and rose up to play.** The word for **play** probably refers to sexual immorality. Such sins usually accompanied idolatry in ancient times. And we know that the Corinthians lived in an especially immoral city and that such sins plagued the church (see 1 Cor. 10:8).

Idolatry was a real temptation for people of ancient times. Idolatry is not practiced in the same way in our culture, but idolatry flourishes. An idol is whatever we give our greatest attention and adoration. Our gods include money, power, popularity, famous people, and many other things; but in the last resort they all are forms of self-worship.

Verse 8 is a specific warning against sexual immorality. **Fornication** translates *porneuo,* from which we get our word *pornography.* The Greek word refers to all kinds of sexual sins. From the large number who perished as a result of this sin, we conclude that Paul had in mind the sin of sexual immorality that took place at Baal-peor, as recorded in Numbers 25. Moabite women infiltrated the Israelite camp and lured the men into worshiping Baal and participating in the sexual immorality that was an integral part of this fertility religion.

The Corinthians had particular trouble resisting temptations to sexual immorality because their city was filled with this sin. Many of the believers had participated in this sin (6:9-11). They had a proud attitude toward the man guilty of incest (5:1-5), and they insisted they were free to determine their own moral values (6:12-13). This shows that some of them felt that sexual immorality was not wrong, at least not for them. Paul's exhortation was to "flee fornication" (6:18). He may have had in mind the example of Joseph who refused Potiphar's wife and fled because he said that adultery was a sin against God (Gen. 39: 9-13). Proverbs warns young men about temptations to commit sexual immorality. The writer of Proverbs 6:27-28 asked: "Can a man take fire in his bosom, and his clothes not be burned? Can one go upon hot coals, and his feet not be burned?" Many a person has thrown away a lifetime of godly living by yielding to this temptation in a moment of weakness!

The Christian religion challenged the sexual depravity of those days, and for centuries traditional Christian values were embraced in many western cultures. Some people still committed these sins, but with the knowledge that they were sinning. Then a sexual revolution swept through the land in the 1960s and sexual standards were turned upside down. Sadly, we have seen our culture return to the sexual wilderness of first-century Corinth. Christians of all ages are often tempted to fall into step with this kind of sin.

Verse 9 says, **Neither let us tempt Christ.** This is a warning against putting Christ to the test. The word **tempt** is *ekpeirazo,* which is used much like *peirazo.* "Test" (NIV) is probably more to the point than **tempt.** Since the Israelites put God to the test more than once while they were in the wilderness, this might refer to several incidents. However, in only one of these incidents were the people **destroyed of serpents.** In Numbers 21:4-9 the Israelites spoke against Moses for bringing them into the wilderness to die. As punishment, the Lord sent fiery serpents among them, killing many of them. The text of Numbers 21:4-9 doesn't refer to the word *test,* but Psalm 78:18 does use the Hebrew equivalent of this word in speaking of this incident.

One of the temptations of Jesus was to put God to the test. He refused (Matt. 4:7). At times the Lord asks us to let Him prove Himself to us (Mal. 3:10). Only in such situations are we justified in doing this. At other times, this is sinful. Notice that Paul warned against putting Christ to the test. This shows two things: First, Christ was involved in the Old Testament events. Second, the Corinthians' idolatry was putting Christ to the test.

First Corinthians 10:10 refers to a time when the Israelites **murmured** against the Lord. Since they grumbled and complained on more than one occasion, several incidents might have been in Paul's mind. One of these is found in Numbers 14, when, after the evil report of the 10 spies, the majority of the children of Israel refused to enter the promised land. The Lord rebuked their grumbling as a sign of their unbelief and disobedience. He sentenced the adults of that generation to wander in the wilderness and to die. None of them over 20 years of age—except for Joshua and Caleb—would ever enter the promised land. By our unbelief and disobedience, we too may miss some of the greatest of God's blessings and fall under His wrath.

Verse 11 repeats some of verse 6 and ties together these four examples. The Scriptures were **written for our admonition** ("warnings," NIV). The Scriptures instruct, encourage, and warn us. We, like the Corinthians, live in "the fulfillment of the ages" (NIV). Because of this, we have the benefit of learning the lessons of those who lived in Old Testament times. The New Testament often uses Old Testament people and events from which to draw lessons for our own age.

1 Corinthians 10:12: **Wherefore let him that thinketh he standeth take heed lest he fall.**

Verse 12 is a warning against overconfidence. Christians are never in so much moral danger as when we assume we are immune from the dangers of temptation. Thus Paul wrote: **Let him that thinketh he standeth take heed lest he fall** ("if you think you are standing firm, be careful that you don't fall!" NIV). This was a warning to those who felt they were free to determine their own moral values or who felt that even if something were wrong they could overcome it in their own strength. Paul warned them against both these dangers in verses 6-12. They were warned against the deadly danger of doing those things that the Lord had forbidden.

Does the word **fall** mean that a believer could fall away from a relationship with God? The word **fall** does not mean that believers fall from grace. However, Jesus made clear that a profession of faith cannot form the only basis for assurance of a relation with the Lord (Matt. 7:21). Those who allow sin to dominate their lives cast great doubt on their claim to be a child of God. Only God knows; but if anyone does what is described in verses 7-10, that person is either lost or severely backslidden. Both are deadly conditions.

What are the lasting lessons from 1 Corinthians 10:6-12?

1. Confidence that we can flirt with temptation and emerge unscathed is a dangerous delusion.

2. We should beware of any temptation to sin against the Lord.

3. Especially dangerous are the temptations to idolatry and to sexual immorality.

4. The Old Testament provides examples that warn us of the dangers of presumption.

Claim God's Promise (1 Cor. 10:13)

*Why did Paul offer this word of encouragement if their problem was presumption? What was his purpose in the first part of verse 13? Why are the words **God is faithful** key to the verse? What promises does God*

*make to those who are tempted? How do we know how much tempta-
tion we are able to endure? How is each **way to escape** suited to the
temptation? What about people who are not looking for a way of escape?*

**1 Corinthians 10:13: There hath no temptation taken you but
such as is common to man: but God is faithful, who will not suffer
you to be tempted above that ye are able; but will with the temptation also make a way to escape, that ye may be able to bear it.**

Why did Paul suddenly insert this word of encouragement in the
midst of warnings against presumption? "The best solution seems to
be to regard it as functioning in two directions at once, both as a con-
tinuation of the warning in vv. 1-12 and as a word of assurance leading to the prohibition to 'flee idolatry' in v. 14. There is no risk of their
falling, he seems to be telling them in response to v. 12, as long as one
is dealing with ordinary trials, God will help them through such."[3]

Paul gave four words of assurance to encourage believers who
wanted to overcome temptation. (1) No one ever faces a totally new
temptation. The word **taken** has the force of "seized" (NIV), implying
that some of the Corinthian believers were struggling with temptations to besetting sins. Some, for example, had lived sexually immoral
lives before their conversions. Their old lives may have had such holds
on them that they were despairing of overcoming their temptations.
Paul reminded them that these were no new temptations and that
others already had overcome them.

(2) **God is faithful.** This is the key word of assurance on which the
others are based. The secret to overcoming temptation is in the faithfulness and strength of God.

(3) The sovereign and holy God does not tempt anyone, and He does
not allow anyone **to be tempted above that** the person is **able** to
endure—with the Lord's help. The unwritten assumption of Paul leads
us to add the words "with the Lord's help." We can't overcome any
temptation on our own. With the Lord's help we can endure what He
allows us to experience. Of course, we cannot presume that God will
provide His power unless we do our part.

(4) God also provides **a way to escape** each temptation. In Greek, the
word **escape** is preceded by "the." This implies that God has a distinctive
way of escape for each temptation—"the way out." This is a wonderful
promise to those seeking how to overcome temptation. God always opens
for us *the way* to escape each temptation. The problem for too many
people is that they never have really decided they want a way to escape.

During the Civil War smuggling from the South to the North was a lucrative but illegal undertaking. One steamboat captain was offered $100 to carry a load of cotton up the river. The captain refused. The man then offered $500, then $1,000, and finally $3,000. The captain refused each offer, and after hearing the offer of $3,000, he drew his gun and said to his tempter, "Get out of this boat. You are coming too near my price."[4] This story illustrates the captain's awareness of his own vulnerability and his willingness to take the way out.

What are the lasting lessons of 1 Corinthians 10:13?

1. No one has a new temptation; every temptation has been faced and overcome.

2. God's faithfulness, not our ability, is the only real basis for assurance.

3. God never allows anyone to be tempted beyond what the person can endure, with the Lord's help.

4. God always offers a way of escape for those who are tempted.

5. We must want to overcome temptation.

❖ *Spiritual Transformations*

James emphasized that none of us can blame God for being tempted because we are tempted by our own evil desires. Paul warned presumptuous people of the dangers of overconfidence. He encouraged the tempted to submit to the faithful God and to take the way of escape offered by God.

This lesson gives three biblical guidelines for resisting temptation. (1) Accept responsibility for our actions and their consequences. (2) Be on guard against presuming on God or on our own strength. (3) Claim God's promise of a way out of temptation.

What are your most frequent or strongest temptations? _____

How do you resist these temptations? _____

Prayer of Commitment: Lord, help me to submit myself to You and to resist the devil. Amen.

[1]Kurt A. Richardson, "James," in *The New American Commentary*, vol. 36 [Nashville: Broadman & Holman Publishers, 1997], 81.

[2]C. Leslie Mitton, *The Epistle of James* [Grand Rapids: William B. Eerdmans Publishing Company, 1966], 46.

[3]Gordon D. Fee, *The First Epistle to the Corinthians*, in The New International Commentary on the New Testament [Grand Rapids: William B. Eerdmans Publishing Company, 1987], 460.

[4]Clarence E. Macartney, *Macartney's Illustrations* [Nashville: Abingdon Press, 1946], 384.

THE PROMISE OF LIFE'S VALUE

Background Passage: Psalm 139:1-24; Mark 10:13-16
Focal Passage: Psalm 139:7-16; Mark 10:13-16
Key Verse: Psalm 139:14

❖ *Significance of the Lesson*

• The *Theme* of this lesson is that God's promise of grace includes His valuing of all human life as sacred.
• The *Life Question* this lesson seeks to address is, Why should I value and protect human life?
• The *Biblical Truth* is that because God created and values all human life, His people are to value and protect human life.
• The *Life Impact* is to help you value and protect human life.
• This is the annual *Sanctity of Human Life Lesson.*

The Value of Human Life

The secular worldview sometimes places a low value on human life. Practices such as abortion, euthanasia, and the neglect and abuse of family members are ways the devaluing of life is shown.

In the biblical worldview, God created and values all human life. Therefore, Christians are to value and protect human life, including unborn children, older adults, and those who suffer from illnesses and infirmities.

The Abortion Debate

This week is the 30th anniversary of Roe vs. Wade, in which the Supreme Court declared abortion legal. Two strongly held views about abortion are hotly debated in our country. These views can best be seen in how two questions are answered. First, when does life begin? Or, to put it another way, is that which is in the mother's womb a person or something less than a person? Second, what effect will termination of the pregnancy have on the mother and on that which is in her womb? Those who favor abortion say that a woman has the right to choose to have an abortion and that the unborn is not a human being. Those who oppose abortion say that abortions not only destroy living humans but also have bad consequences (physical, emotional, spiritual) for many women who have an abortion.

Word Study: *Blessed*

The word **blessed** in Mark 10:16 describes what Jesus did for the little children. The Greek word is *kateulogeo.* The root word means "to speak well of someone" or "to speak well to someone." In this case it means that Jesus called on God to show His goodness in the lives of these children. Thus it was a form of prayer.

❖ *Search the Scriptures*

Since God is present everywhere, no one can escape His presence. God is active in the creation and development of new human life within the womb. Jesus rebuked those who discouraged children being brought to Him.

The Spirit's Presence (Ps. 139:7-12)

What is the theme and outline of Psalm 139? When do people seek to flee from God? Why is this foolish and futile? Are these verses disturbing or encouraging?

Psalm 139:7-12: Whither shall I go from thy spirit? or whither shall I flee from thy presence? [8]If I ascend up into heaven, thou art there: if I make my bed in hell, behold, thou art there. [9]If I take the wings of the morning, and dwell in the uttermost parts of the sea; [10]even there shall thy hand lead me, and thy right hand shall hold me. [11]If I say, Surely the darkness shall cover me; even the night shall be light about me. [12]Yea, the darkness hideth not from thee; but the night shineth as the day: the darkness and the light are both alike to thee.

The theme of Psalm 139 is the greatness of God. Theologians speak of the aspects of God's greatness as omniscience, omnipresence, and omnificence. These are big words for knowing all things, being present at all places, and creating all things. Derek Kidner outlined the psalm this way: The All-Seeing (vv. 1-6), The All-Present (vv. 7-12), The All-Creative (vv. 13-18), and The All-Holy (vv. 19-24).[1] Thus one characteristic of the psalm is its deep theological meaning. Another characteristic is its personal style. H. C. Leupold noted: "The thinking in evidence in this psalm is not formulated in theological abstractions but in terms of personal religious experience: the psalm throbs with warm emotion and deep feeling."[2]

Some people deny there is a God, or, if there is, they claim He either does not know or does not care about human beings. They base this on the pain, injustice, and evil in the world. The Bible affirms that God knows and cares. One such affirmation is in Psalm 139:1-6, in which the psalmist wrote that God knew and understood everything about him. He confessed that he could not understand God, but he knew that God understood him.

In verses 7-12 the psalmist affirmed that God is present with us wherever we go. The two questions in verse 7 show that some people seek to **flee from** God's **presence.** The psalmist may have tried to do that at some point in his life. David certainly tried to hide from God after his two terrible sins. This attempt to flee and to hide from God goes back to Adam and Eve, who tried to hide from the Lord among the trees of the garden. The very nature of sin is to turn our backs on God and go the other way. Efforts to flee from God are futile and foolish. They are futile because, as verses 8-12 show, finding a place without God is impossible. Jonah tried to flee from God, but God sought and found him. Fleeing from God is foolish because, as we see in verse 10, His purpose is to guide and assure us.

Before leaving verse 7, notice that this is an example of synonymous parallelism in Hebrew poetry. Each question means the same thing although different words are used. One thing to notice about verse 7 is that the words **spirit** and **presence** are parallel. This shows that the Spirit of God is the way we refer to the presence of God. This is a consistent biblical teaching. The Spirit of God is the presence of God at work in our lives and in our world. Verses 8-12 emphasize that we cannot escape the all-pervasive presence of the Spirit of God.

Beginning with verse 8, the psalmist examined various human ways of trying to get away from God and showed why they all fail. First, he imagined if he was able to **ascend up into heaven** and at the opposite extreme to **make** his **bed in hell** ("in Sheol," NASB; "in the depths," NIV). Several words are translated **hell** in the *King James Version*.

Some of these words refer only to the place of the dead; others refer to the place of eternal punishment. The word as used in verse 8 refers to the realm beyond death.

Verse 9 is a way of saying that if I moved with the speed of light to a distant place, I would find God already there. No place in this world or in outer space is without the presence of the Creator.

Verse 10 shows why we should welcome the presence of God with us at all times. The assurance grows out of the fact that the **hand** of God will **lead** us and His **right hand** will **hold** us. To **lead** is to guide. To **hold** is to protect and keep secure. Fleeing from God is foolish because His is a hand of love. The writer of Psalm 73 testified: "I am continually with thee: thou hast holden me by my right hand. Thou shalt guide me with thy counsel, and afterward receive me to glory" (vv. 23-24).

Verses 11-12 return to the theme of the futility of trying to flee from God. The psalmist imagined himself in the deepest **darkness**. Many evil acts are done in the dark of the night. People seem to feel they are unseen in the darkness. Just as people can see in the dark with special night lens, so has God always been able to see. The writer was aware that no one can hide from God in the darkness, for **the night shineth as the day** because of the presence of God.

What are the lasting lessons in Psalm 139:7-12?

1. The Spirit of God is the presence of God.

2. Trying to flee from God is foolish because God is seeking us in love.

3. Trying to flee from God is futile because no one can escape His presence.

The Creator's Plan (Ps. 139:13-16)

Are conception and development within the womb purely biological or is God involved? What four words describe God's work within the womb? How is the unborn described in these verses? How did the psalmist praise God for how he was made? How is God's purpose for an unborn child described? What implications do these verses have for the abortion issue?

Psalm 139:13-16: **For thou hast possessed my reins: thou hast covered me in my mother's womb. [14]I will praise thee; for I am fearfully and wonderfully made: marvelous are thy works; and that my soul knoweth right well. [15]My substance was not hid from thee, when I was made in secret, and curiously wrought in the lowest parts of the earth. [16]Thine eyes did see my substance, yet being**

unperfect; and in thy book all my members were written, which in continuance were fashioned, when as yet there was none of them.

Since this is one of the most important Bible passages with bearing on abortion, we will look carefully at it to be sure we understand its message. The overall message of these verses is that God created new life within the womb and that He has a purpose for each new life. There are five main points to notice. The five points answer five questions: *who, how, where, what,* and *why?*

For one thing, God is the One *who* is the Creator of human life. He created Adam and Eve in a unique way in the beginning, and He continues His creative work in each new life conceived and developed within the womb. Conception and birth are not purely biological processes. Mother Nature does not do it. The eternal God does it. The fact that God is the Creator is crucial.

Second, four terms are used in verses 13 and 15 to describe *how* God forms human life. **Hast possessed** translates *qana* and means "formed" (NASB, NRSV) or "created" (NIV). **Covered me** translates *sakak* and can mean "knit me together" (NIV; NRSV). This word is found in Job 10:11, "clothe me with skin and flesh and knit me together with bones and sinews" (NIV). The verb has the idea of God as a weaver in His creative work within the womb. This word is similar in meaning to *raqam,* which is translated **curiously wrought** in verse 15. Many translators see the meaning of weaving or embroidering in this word—"woven together" (NIV) or "intricately woven" (NRSV). This word is found numerous times of the work of those who constructed the tabernacle according to God's instructions. Exodus 26:36, for example, refers to "the work of a weaver" (NASB). The other word in verse 15 is **made,** which translates *'asah,* a word used throughout the Old Testament for the continuing creative work of the Lord. Psalm 100:3 reminds us that "it is he that hath made us, and not we ourselves."

The combination of these four words shows that God is the One who creates human life within the womb. He is pictured as a skillful weaver who puts together the complex parts of the human body. This focuses our attention on the third question about *where* this work is done. The psalmist wrote that God's creative work in making him took place **in my mother's womb.** Verse 15 refers to the place as **the lowest parts of the earth** ("the depths of the earth," NIV). These words "are a metaphor for deepest concealment, *i.e.,* the hiddenness of the womb."[3] All of this creative work of God takes place within the womb.

The answer to *what* is found in the words translated **reins** and **substance. Reins** refers to the kidneys. In Hebrew psychology, this idiom referred to the seat of human emotions and moral sensitivity, that is, to one's "inmost being" (NIV) or "inward parts" (NASB, NRSV, NKJV, REB, NEB). **Substance** is usually translated "frame" (NASB, NKJV, NIV, NRSV). The word *'osem* means "strength" or "bones." The reference may be to the skeletal structure of the body.

Verse 14 is the psalmist's personal testimony of his belief about his creation within his mother's womb. He praised God because, as he said, **I am fearfully and wonderfully made.** Since the context deals with creation within the womb, the writer was thinking of the divine work on him before his birth. In those days they lacked the technology to watch the development of life within the womb. If he could have seen how life develops step by step, he would only more loudly affirmed what he wrote. Human characteristics appear early after conception. On day 20 foundations of the brain, spinal cord, and nervous system already are established. On day 21 the heart begins to beat. On day 28 the backbone and muscles are forming. Arms, legs, eyes, and ears have begun to show. By day 30 the new life is 10,000 times larger than the fertilized egg.[4]

Verse 16 helps to answer the *why* question. The words **all my members** is literally "all of them." The word "them" is seen in two different ways. The *King James Version* assumes that it refers back to **substance,** hence to the development of the new life within the womb. The *New International Version* (similarly NKJV, NASB, NRSV) understands "all of them" to refer to the days of one's life. The first line of verse 16 reinforces verses 13-15, but the last part seems to make a related point: that before our birth God knows all about the days of our lives.

> Even before I was born,
> you had written in your book
> everything I would do" (CEV).

This mention of purpose is consistent with Jeremiah 1:5, in which the Lord told Jeremiah,

> Before I formed you in the womb I knew you,
> before you were born I set you apart;
> I appointed you as a prophet to the nations (NIV).

The two main points of Psalm 139:13-16 are: (1) God creates human life within the womb, and (2) He has a purpose for each life.

This passage has several crucial implications that relate to abortion. For one thing, God is seen as the Creator of ongoing human life through human procreation. Bible passages show that God is involved in conception as well as development within the womb. God not only created the first man and woman, but He also commissioned them and their descendants to be co-creators with Him of ongoing human life. Every birth is a miracle. The sense of this miracle is not diminished by modern technology, which enables parents to view images of the preborn child as he or she is developing within the mother.

Scott Klusendorf, a pro-life advocate and debater, said that the abortion issue is not morally complex but basically simple. He illustrated this by asking parents to imagine that their child came up behind the parent and asked, "Can I kill this?" The parent would turn around to see what "this" is before answering. What is "this" within the womb of a pregnant woman? Is this a human being or is this something less than human? Klusendorf supported his pro-life position by applying what he called the SLED test. How does a newborn child differ from one still in the womb? An unborn child differs from a newborn one in only four ways—none of which denies its status as a human being. None of these differences is significant enough to justify killing the unborn.

• *Size*: Large people are not more human than small people.

• *Level of development*: Is a four-year-old girl who has yet to develop her reproductive system less human than a 21-year-old?

• *Environment*: *Where* you are has no bearing on *who* you are. Being outside the womb does not transform something less than human into a human being.

• *Dependency*: If viability is what makes us human, then all those who depend on kidney machines or heart pacemakers are non-human.[5]

If one asks the child's question concerning a preborn child, the right and logical answer is no, you must not kill this because this is a human being.

What are the lasting lessons of Psalm 139:13-16?

1. God is involved in conception and in the development of life within the womb. These things are not purely biological in nature.

2. The unborn child is a human being.

3. God creates each person in the womb and endows each with the same image of God given to the first human beings.

4. God has a purpose for people before they are born.

5. None of the differences between an unborn child and a newborn baby is significant enough to consider the unborn child to be less than human.

6. Since the unborn child is a human being, that life is to be nurtured and protected, not threatened or taken.

The Savior's Touch (Mark 10:13-16)

Why were parents bringing their children to Jesus? Why did the disciples rebuke them? How did Jesus feel about this? What did He teach about entering the kingdom? What did He do for the children? What implications do these verses have for the abortion issue?

Mark 10:13-16: And they brought young children to him, that he should touch them: and his disciples rebuked those that brought them. [14]But when Jesus saw it, he was much displeased, and said unto them, Suffer the little children to come unto me, and forbid them not: for of such is the kingdom of God. [15]Verily I say unto you, Whosoever shall not receive the kingdom of God as a little child, he shall not enter therein. [16]And he took them up in his arms, put his hands upon them, and blessed them.

Appropriately, Mark placed this familiar incident right after His teachings on marriage (10:1-12). The people who **brought young children** *(paidia)* to Jesus were probably their parents. "The word translated 'children' could refer to any age between infancy and twelve (cf. its use in 5:39,42 to refer to a twelve-year-old girl). Verse 16, however, suggests that these children were small."[6] The parents wanted Him to **touch them.** They knew that the touch of Jesus was a healing, blessing, and life-giving touch.

These parents were doing the right thing in bringing their children to Jesus. Modern parents would do well to follow their example. Jesus loves children, and children often easily love Jesus. Parents owe this to their children. Some parents say that they are not indoctrinating their children because they want their children later to be able to make their own decisions about faith or unbelief. The problem with this is that the world will be all that the person knows about. Christ will be left out by default.

Parents who bring their children to Jesus often encounter difficulties and barriers, but the barriers ought not to be the adult disciples of Jesus. Yet we read that it was His disciples who **rebuked those**

that brought the children. What led the disciples to do that? Perhaps they felt that Jesus' time was too precious to spend it with little children. Perhaps they felt that the children were too young to understand and appreciate who Jesus was.

Whatever their excuse, **when Jesus saw it, he was much displeased** ("indignant," NIV, NASB). The word is *aganakteo,* which comes from two words meaning "much grief." The word expresses anger growing out of pain or sorrow. Jesus at times grew angry. It was usually when someone was exploited or someone's needs were not being met. These parents and the children wanted to see Jesus, and He was angry with the disciples for turning them away with a rebuke.

The disciples had turned them away, but Jesus reminded His disciples that any adult who entered **the kingdom of God** had to do so **as a little child.** Jesus then gave standing orders to allow **little children to come unto** Him. No one was to hinder their coming, **for of such is the kingdom of God.** Anyone who enters the kingdom must have the openness, humility, and trust of a child.

Then Jesus **took them up in his arms, put his hands upon them, and blessed them.** Little children can sense when adults really care about them and when they do not. These children correctly recognized that Jesus truly loved them. Some adults do not place high priority on little children and those who lovingly care for them. Previously Jesus had told the disciples, "Whoever welcomes one of these little children in my name welcomes me" (Mark 9:36, NIV). In loving little children, Jesus was revealing the heart of the Heavenly Father. He said, "See that you do not look down on one of these little ones. For I tell you that their angels in heaven always see the face of my Father in heaven" (Matt. 18:10, NIV).

The first-century world was not a children's world. Unwanted infants were killed or exposed and left to die. They often died of exposure, sickness, hunger, or thirst. Sometimes an evil person would take the helpless infant for diabolical purposes. Abortion also was an accepted part of pagan society. No wonder the early Christians opposed all of these ways of mistreating children. They opposed infanticide and abortion because they believed in the precious gift of life that God was seeking to give to the unborn and newborn child.

What are the lasting truths in Mark 10:13-16?

1. Parents should bring their children to Jesus.

2. Sometimes adults discourage parents from bringing their children to Jesus.

3. Turning aside little children displeases the Lord.

4. The only door to God's kingdom is to come like a little child.

5. We should protect the lives and welfare of unborn and newborn babies.

❖ *Spiritual Transformations*

Trying to escape the presence of God is futile and foolish. It is futile because it is impossible to escape One who is present everywhere. It is foolish because God seeks us in love. God is involved in the conception and development of preborn life within the womb. He has a purpose for each unborn child. When parents brought little children, the disciples rebuked them. Jesus was angry with the disciples; He welcomed and blessed the little children.

The Life Impact of this lesson is to help you value and protect human life. The valuing of human life is something that involves the mind and heart. The protecting of human life involves acting on behalf of those unable to protect themselves. Children of God seek to live by the teachings of God's Word. Have you allowed Him to speak to you on this subject? What is your understanding of Psalm 139:13-16 and Jeremiah 1:5? Are your values based on the Scriptures? We must ask ourselves these questions on every issue of life.

What value do you place on the life of an unborn baby? _____

What opportunities for protecting new life do you have? _____

Do you have a crisis pregnancy center in your area? How do you support their work? _____

Prayer of Commitment: Dear Lord, giver of life, watch over and protect those whose lives are threatened, and use me to be Your instrument in this. Amen.

[1]Derek Kidner, *Psalms 73–150*, in the Tyndale Old Testament Commentaries [Downers Grove: InterVarsity Press, 1975], 464-467.

[2]H. C. Leupold, *Exposition of the Psalms* [Grand Rapids: Baker Book House, 1969], 942.

[3]Kidner, *Psalms 73–150*, 466.

[4]*The First Nine Months* (Colorado Springs: Focus on the Family, 1993), 4.

[5]Scott DeNicola, "Recruiting the Next Generation," in *Focus on the Family Citizen*, January 2000, 19-20.

[6]James A. Brooks, "Mark," in *The New American Commentary*, vol. 23 [Nashville: Broadman Press, 1991], 159.

THE PROMISE OF HEAVEN

Background Passage: John 14:1-4; Revelation 21:1–22:6
Focal Passage: John 14:1-4; Revelation 21:1-5; 22:1-5
Key Verse: John 14:2

❖ *Significance of the Lesson*

• The *Theme* of this lesson is that God's promise of grace includes a future place in Jesus' presence.
• The *Life Question* this lesson seeks to address is, What kind of place is heaven?
• The *Biblical Truth* is that God has promised believers a future place in heaven.
• The *Life Impact* is to help you live each day in anticipation of heaven.

Views About Heaven

Some adults deny any kind of life after death. Many focus only on this life and consider talk of heaven irrelevant. Some see an afterlife as a pie-in-the-sky promise. Others assume that everyone will be in some kind of afterlife.

In the biblical worldview, heaven is a reality for which believers confidently hope based on the promises of God and the resurrection of Jesus from the dead.

Word Study: *mansions*

The Greek word translated **mansions** is found only in John 14:2,23. It is used in the singular in verse 23 and in the plural in verse 2. It means a dwelling place, either temporary or permanent. At least one Greek writer used the word to describe the rest stops on a journey. Those who interpret John 14:2 in this way understand Jesus to have been referring either to stages in the pilgrimage of faith or to levels of progression in the heavens. Most Bible students, however, believe that

Jesus was referring to permanent dwelling places. This is based on three reasons: Jesus used it this way in verse 23, where it is translated "abode." The related verb means "to remain" or "to abide." The context of the verse favors permanent dwelling places. The word **mansions** actually comes from the Latin Vulgate, which used the Latin word for dwelling place *(mansiones).*

❖ *Search the Scriptures*

Jesus told His disciples that although He was going away, He was going to prepare a place for them. He also promised to come back and take them to be with Him. The new heavens and new earth will be a new place with new conditions, including leaving behind all that blights life on earth. In the new place, believers will see God and serve Him forever.

The Focal Passage Outline provides three answers to the Life Question: What kind of place is heaven?

A Place Prepared by Jesus (John 14:1-4)

*What was troubling the disciples? What is God's **house**? What are the **many mansions**? How was Jesus going **to prepare a place** for His followers? Was He promising to come for them at death or at His second coming?*

John 14:1-4: Let not your heart be troubled: ye believe in God, believe also in me. **²In my Father's house are many mansions: if it were not so, I would have told you. I go to prepare a place for you. ³And if I go and prepare a place for you, I will come again, and receive you unto myself; that where I am, there ye may be also. ⁴And whither I go ye know, and the way ye know.**

Be troubled is the opposite of peace, for Jesus said: "Peace I leave with you, my peace I give unto you: not as the world giveth, give I unto you. Let not your heart be troubled, neither let it be afraid" (v. 27). Jesus had just told His disciples that He was going away (13:33,36). Thus Jesus said, **Let not your heart be troubled.**

Believe can be either a statement or a command. Many Bible students think that Jesus intended both uses in verse 1 to be commands or imperatives: "Trust in God; trust also in me" (NIV); "Believe in God, believe also in Me" (NRSV, HCSB). In other words, trust both the Father and the Son.

Jesus used the word **my** to describe His personal relationship with God the Father. Through Jesus we also can call God "our Father" (Matt. 6:9). Jesus was about to go back to His Father, and He was making the disciples a promise about the **Father's house. House** (oikos) can refer to a building or a family. Here it was used by Jesus to refer to heaven. Jesus said that His Father's house contains **many mansions.** As used here, the Greek word refers to permanent "dwelling places" (NASB, NRSV, HCSB). If we think of **house** as the entire place called heaven, the dwelling places may be thought of as separate dwellings in God's country. If we think of all of heaven as God's **house,** or as His dwelling, the idea may be "in my Father's house are many rooms" (NIV). The point is that in heaven there is plenty of room for all God's children.

Jesus affirmed the truthfulness of His words by saying, **If it were not so, I would have told you.** Then He continued by making two great promises. The first one is, **I go to prepare a place for you.** Notice that Jesus referred to heaven as **a place.** Jesus said that He was going **to prepare** this **place.** And this preparation was to be **for you**—for His followers. What did Jesus do to prepare a place for us? We know what He did while still in the flesh. He went to the cross and laid down His life for us. And He was raised from the dead. Together these saving events offered forgiveness of sins and victory over death for believers. Thus Jesus made possible our entry into the Father's house. He is our intercessor who sits at the right hand of God. He no doubt did other things that prepared heaven for us and us for heaven. As someone said, "Heaven is a prepared place for a prepared people."

The other side of this promise is that Jesus promised to **come again, and receive you unto myself.** The primary reference is to His future coming, when Jesus will come for His people. This future coming is the key event in the end-time events. Living believers and the dead in Christ look forward to this time of reunion of all God's children as the prelude to the new heavens and new earth. Yet this text is also often used in funerals and in ministering to the sick and dying. In a sense, the Lord comes to each believer at death and takes the believer to Himself.

Where is this place with the Lord? We don't know the answers to all the questions about heaven, but we do know two things: First, we know that it is a real place. Second, we know that it is to be with Jesus Christ in a place He has prepared for us in our Father's house.

Jesus told the disciples that they knew **the way.** Thomas protested that they did not know where He was going or the way to get there (v. 5). This set the stage for one of the great "I am" statements of Jesus in verse 6: "I am the way, the truth, and the life: no man cometh unto the Father, but by me."

Sometimes a family moves to a new location many miles away. The father often goes ahead of the rest of the family. He prepares for their coming in many ways. Then he goes back and brings the rest of the family to the newly prepared place. Jesus did this, only much more.

What are the lasting lessons in John 14:1-4?

1. The peace that Christ gives calms our troubled hearts.
2. Heaven is our Heavenly Father's house.
3. There is room in the Father's house for all who know Christ.
4. Jesus went away to prepare a place in heaven for each one.
5. He promised to come again to take His own to be with Him.
6. Heaven is to be with Christ.

A Place Where Everything Is Made New (Rev. 21:1-5)

Will the new heaven and the new earth be a renovation of the present universe or a totally new one? What is the significance of the **new Jerusalem, coming down from God**? *How are the new Jerusalem and the* **bride** *related? What did John see and what did he hear? What is the meaning of verse 3? What unpleasant aspects of the present earth will not be in the new one?*

Revelation 21:1-2: And I saw a new heaven and a new earth: for the first heaven and the first earth were passed away; and there was no more sea. ²And I John saw the holy city, new Jerusalem, coming down from God out of heaven, prepared as a bride adorned for her husband.

Revelation 21–22 tells of the positive side of the eternal state. Revelation 20:10-15 describes the judgment and the casting of Satan, death and the grave, and all those whose names are not written in the Lamb's book of life into the lake of fire. Both heaven and hell are realities. The description of the eternal punishment of the lost stands in stark contrast to the description of the eternal life of the saved. Revelation 21:1-5 introduces a long section on heaven. Verses 1-2 tell what John **saw**; verses 3-5 tell what he **heard.**

John **saw a new heaven and a new earth.** Two Greek words for *new* are used in the New Testament. *Kainos* refers to new in quality; *neos* refers to new in time. The word here is *kainos.* This doesn't clearly show whether the new heaven and new earth will be renovations of the old or whether they will be totally new after the destruction of the old. There is some evidence for both points of view. In favor of the renovation view are passages such as Romans 8:19-22, where Paul wrote of the renewal of the old creation. In support for the other view is 2 Peter 3:7,10-13, where Peter described the destruction of the old creation. In favor of the renovation view is the mention of earthly things such as an earth and a city; but on the other hand, the new creation will have no sea, no night, and no sun. We also have the description in Revelation 20:11: "I saw a great white throne, and him that sat on it, from whose face the earth and the heaven fled away; and there was found no place for them." The same idea is communicated here in 21:1 by the words **were passed away** ("had vanished," NEB, REB).

Suppose a family decided they needed a new house. They might build a totally new house, or they might totally renovate the old one into a new house. In either case, they would have what amounts to a new house. We don't know which God will do, but one thing is for sure: everything will be **new—Behold, I make all things new** (v. 5).

Another thing to keep in mind is this: The new heaven and the new earth will be a place, not a state of mind. It will be corporeal or substantive. It will not be like a cloud into which people merge like mist rising.

The reference to **no more sea** has at least two points. For one thing, to the Israelites, the sea was a place of danger and unrest (Isa. 57:20). The ships of that day were small, and many were lost at sea. The other meaning is that the sea stood for separation. John was in exile on an island, separated from his beloved brothers and sisters on the mainland. For him, **no more sea** may have included the idea of "no more separation."

John also **saw the holy city, new Jerusalem.** The old Jerusalem was gone. It had played a key role in the years before the end, but now its heavenly counterpart is pictured as coming. This will be a truly **holy city.** A lengthy description of it is found in Revelation 21:9–22:5. Here it is described as **coming down from God out of heaven.** These are significant words. The new city is a gift of God's grace, not the result of human accomplishment. Humans have tried to build utopias on earth and have always failed. We cannot build or earn heaven; we can only receive it by repentance and faith in Christ. The New Testament often emphasizes that the Christian hope is for a holy, heavenly city (see Gal. 4:25-26; Heb. 11:16; 12:22; 13:14). The Book of Hebrews uses the analogy of earthly life as being a pilgrimage of faith to this heavenly city. John Bunyan put this into allegory form in *The Pilgrim's Progress.*

The new heavenly city is closely related to the **bride.** In verse 2 the city is **prepared as a bride adorned for her husband. Prepared** is the same word Jesus used in John 14:2. In Revelation 21:9, an angel told John, "Come hither, and I will show thee the bride, the Lamb's wife." Then the angel showed him the holy city (v. 10). This almost identifies the bride and the city. However, the probable meaning is that the city is the place in which the bride resides. An invitation to the wedding supper of the Lamb was issued in 19:6-9; the wedding seems to be described in Revelation 21. The bride is the church. Christ is the groom. The metaphor of marriage stresses the intimacy of the relationship between God and His redeemed people.

Revelation 21:3-5: **And I heard a great voice out of heaven saying, Behold, the tabernacle of God is with men, and he will dwell with them, and they shall be his people, and God himself shall be with them, and be their God. ⁴And God shall wipe away all tears from their eyes; and there shall be no more death, neither sorrow, nor crying, neither shall there be any more pain: for the former things are passed away. ⁵And he that sat upon the throne said, Behold, I make all things new. And he said unto me, Write: for these words are true and faithful.**

The intimacy of the marriage metaphor is continued in the use of **the tabernacle of God. Tabernacle,** or "dwelling place," is *skene.* **He will dwell with them,** or "he will tabernacle with them," has the related verb *skenosei.* This word has its roots in the Old Testament Shekinah glory of God, which denoted the glorious presence of God with His people first in the tabernacle and later in the temple. The last part of verse 3 is a fulfillment of Old Testament promises such as Ezekiel 37:27. As the prophets had foretold, **they shall be his people, and God himself shall be with them, and be their God.**

Verse 4 is a favorite verse for many believers. It describes some of the unpleasant parts of earthly existence that will not be in the new heaven and the new earth. We wonder what heaven will be like. The

Bible does not satisfy our curiosity, but it gives us two kinds of answers to the question. Both kinds of answers take into account that we humans have no basis in our experience for God to be able to communicate much about heaven with us. Therefore, He uses our earthly experiences to describe heaven.

God tells us that heaven is like having a permanent room in the Father's house or a dwelling in His country. It is like the joy of a wedding. It is like cool refreshing water when you are thirsty. It is like a beautiful garden. In verses 9-22 God describes heaven as a holy city having streets of gold, gates of pearls, and walls of precious jewels. He took things and experiences that people on earth consider most joyful and valuable, and He used them to reveal what heaven will be like. He was saying that it will be wonderful beyond our highest hopes.

But God had another way of communicating to humans what heaven will be like. In verse 4 John heard the good news of what will not be in the new heaven and new earth. He listed some of the most dreaded aspects of earthly existence. Gone will be all **sorrow** and **crying. God shall wipe away all tears from their eyes.** There may be tears of joy, but no tears of grief, loneliness, despair, or guilt. Two of the worst aspects of earthly existence will not be there: **pain** and **death.** All the sufferers of pain and disabilities will be set free from their plights. Pain and death are consequences of the fall of humans into sin. Death and the grave, along with Satan, will be cast into the lake of fire (20:10,13-14). Because of this, in the new heaven and new earth there will be no more death. In the future, the original paradise of God will be restored (see 22:1-3).

Verse 5 records what God Himself said. After reinforcing His promise to **make all things new,** God said to John, **Write: for these words are true and faithful.**

Vachel Lindsay wrote a poem titled "General William Booth Enters into Heaven." Booth was the founder of the Salvation Army. He gave himself to save the hopeless cases of the London slums. In his old age he lost his sight but continued to serve. The poet pictured heaven as being like a county court house square. The following words describe the transformation of the maimed as they meet Jesus.

> Jesus came from out the court-house door,
> Stretched his hands above the passing poor.
> Booth saw not, but led his queer ones there
> Round and round the mighty court-house square.

Then, in an instant all that blear review
Marched on spotless, clad in raiment new.
The lame were straightened, withered limbs uncurled
And blind eyes opened on a new, sweet world.[1]

What are the lasting lessons of Revelation 21:1-5?

1. Heaven and hell are realities.
2. The new heaven and new earth is the eternal state of believers.
3. The people of God are the bride of Christ.
4. God will be there with His people.
5. Tears, weeping, mourning, pain, and death will not be there.

A Place of Serving and Seeing God (Rev. 22:1-5)

*What is the **river of water of life**? How do these verses reverse Genesis 3? What will believers do in heaven? Why is seeing God the supreme good of the godly?*

Revelation 22:1-5: And he showed me a pure river of water of life, clear as crystal, proceeding out of the throne of God and of the Lamb. [2]In the midst of the street of it, and on either side of the river, was there the tree of life, which bare twelve manner of fruits, and yielded her fruit every month: and the leaves of the tree were for the healing of the nations. [3]And there shall be no more curse: but the throne of God and of the Lamb shall be in it; and his servants shall serve him: [4]and they shall see his face; and his name shall be in their foreheads. [5]And there shall be no night there; and they need no candle, neither light of the sun; for the Lord God giveth them light: and they shall reign forever and ever.

Genesis 3 tells how sin entered the world. God had offered Adam and Eve all the trees of the garden, including the tree of life. After their sin, God pronounced the curse of pain and toil on them. Worst of all, they lost access to the tree of life. They thus lost the paradise God offered them and brought on themselves and their descendants a sinful and imperfect world. Revelation 22:1-5 describes the reverse of Genesis 3. For one thing, those in the new city will have access to **the tree of life.** The description actually is of life-giving trees **on either side of the river. The river** itself is identified as **a pure river of water of life. Life** is the prominent word in both of these—**the tree of life** and the **water of life.** The **life** represents the continuous, abundant, and eternal life that will be central in the new heaven and new earth.

God is the source of this life. Ezekiel 47 describes a river flowing from the temple, bringing life to the desert and even to the Dead Sea. The river of Revelation 22:1 flows from **the throne of God and of the Lamb.** This expression refers to the visions of Revelation 4–5. The point is that the water flows from God and His Son. The water signifies the life-giving presence of God in and among His people.

No more curse refers back to the curse of sin in Genesis 3:14-19. The reversal of this curse means the end of pain and toil and of the sin that caused them (see also Rom. 8:19-22).

The presence of God with His people is the central reality of Revelation 21:1–22:5. This is seen in 21:3 in which God dwells among His people. Thus no temple is needed in the new city (21:22). And then here in 22:3 we read, **The throne of God and of the Lamb shall be in it.** There will be no need for the **light of the sun** because **the Lord God giveth them light.**

What will the residents of the new city do? These verses emphasize two things: **his servants shall serve him** and **they shall see his face.** Prior to this time, no human could see the face of God and live (Ex. 33:20). God revealed Himself in His Son in a way that anyone who has seen the Son has seen God's revelation in a person (John 1:14; 14:9). Yet Jesus promised that the pure in heart would see God (Matt. 5:8). This is the highest good or goal of true believers. It will become a reality in the new world. Seeing God means unrestricted sight of Him and His presence.

The word **servants** is *douloi,* or "slaves." **Shall serve** is *latreusousin.* This word usually refers to religious service. In the Greek version of the Old Testament it was used to refer to the service of priests. In the New Testament it sometimes has a more general meaning (Rom. 1:9; 2 Tim. 1:3). No priests will be needed to offer sacrifices in heaven, and there will be no temple. God called Israel as a whole to be a kingdom of priests, a role the nation failed to perform. Christians inherited this commission (1 Pet. 2:9; Rev. 1:6). This role will be perfected in the new heaven and new earth.

What kind of service will be involved? Worship will be the heart of this service, but may it not also include other ways of serving Him? The Bible speaks of rest and work in 14:13. Thus heaven will be a time of rest from our labors and toils, but perhaps a new beginning of that kind of work that glorifies God. In the parable of the talents, the good and faithful servants were rewarded with a larger stewardship

(Matt. 25:21,23). This implies that heaven will provide opportunities for growth and service. "Eternity will never be boring. We cannot imagine exactly what it will mean for us to serve and worship God throughout eternity or even that he would desire such. The implication, however, is of great activity, not passive lethargy."[2]

> When earth's last picture is painted, and the tubes are twisted and dried,
> When the oldest colors have faded, and the youngest critic has died,
> We shall rest, and, faith, we shall need it—lie down for an aeon or two,
> Till the Master of All Good Workmen shall put us to work anew.[3]

What are the lasting lessons of Revelation 22:1-5?
1. The paradise lost in Genesis 3 will be restored in Revelation 22.
2. God will provide continuous life.
3. God will be the central feature of the new creation.
4. Believers will see God.
5. Believers will serve God.

❖ Spiritual Transformations

Jesus promised to prepare a place for us and to come again to take us to be with Him. The new heaven and new earth will have none of the things that blight our present earthly existence. In the new city we will see God and serve Him.

Do you live each day in anticipation of heaven? This doesn't mean gazing upward. It means to live now in light of your confident hope of heaven.

How do you live by heaven's standards in this world? _____
_____

What feature of heaven is most precious to you? _____

Prayer of Commitment: Lord, thank You for the assurance of heaven through Jesus Christ. Help me to live and speak as a citizen of Your eternal kingdom. Amen.

[1]Vachel Lindsay, "General William Booth Enters into Heaven," in *Masterpieces of Religious Verse*, 503.

[2]Kendell H. Easley, "Revelation," in the *Holman New Testament Commentary* [Nashville: Broadman & Holman Publishers, 1998], 415-416.

[3]Rudyard Kipling, "L'Envoi," in *Masterpieces of Religious Verse*, 602.

Study Theme

The Bible: God's Book of Grace

"Returning to his home in Germany, a repatriated prisoner of the Russians brought a strange and eloquent treasure—a complete New Testament, copied by hand on paper salvaged from old cement sacks. Laboriously, dangerously, in hours snatched after terrible days of enforced labor, the prisoners had made ten of these cement sack testaments, and used them in worship."[1] Why did these prisoners take such risks to make these rough copies of the New Testament? They did it because they realized that this book is like no other. God spoke to them through this book.

Two hunters became lost while hunting. They stopped at an old cabin. One of the hunters noticed an unusual doorstop. It was an old book. In fact, it was a rare edition of the *King James Version*. The hunter asked the family about it. The man said, "Oh, Pa give it to me. His pa give it to him." This particular copy was worth thousands of dollars as a rare book, and worth more to all who hear and heed the Word of God. But this family saw it only as a doorstop.[2] Whether from ignorance or indifference, this family failed to recognize the value of the Bible.

This four-session study focuses our attention on "The Bible: God's Book of Grace." The first lesson, "The Bible: Its Origin," is based on Hebrews 1:1-2 and 2 Peter 1:12-21. The second lesson, "The Bible: Its Value," is based on verses from Psalm 119 and Jeremiah 36. The third lesson, "The Bible: Its Purpose," is based on Psalm 19:7-14 and 2 Timothy 3:14-17. The fourth lesson, "The Bible: Its Testimony," is based on verses from John 5 and Acts 17.

This study is designed to help you

• affirm the Bible as God's inspired Word (Feb. 2)
• treasure the Bible (Feb. 9)
• live by biblical standards (Feb. 16)
• regularly study the Scriptures to learn about and follow Jesus (Feb. 23)

[1]Merrill R. Abbey, *Encounter with Christ* [Nashville: Abingdon Press, 1961], 105.
[2]Dick O'Brien, "The Door Prop," *The Beam*, September 1963, 37.

THE BIBLE: ITS ORIGIN

Bible Passage: Hebrews 1:1-2; 2 Peter 1:12-21
Key Verses: 2 Peter 1:20-21

❖ *Significance of the Lesson*

• The *Theme* of this lesson is that the Holy Bible was written by men divinely inspired and is God's revelation of Himself to humanity.
• The *Life Question* this lesson seeks to address is, How did we get the Bible?
• The *Biblical Truth* is that the Bible originated from God.
• The *Life Impact* is to help you affirm the Bible as God's inspired Word.

Views on the Bible

In the secular worldview, the Bible is often viewed as nothing more than a book of literature written by human authors. At best this view attributes the Bible's origin to people recording their religious reflections, insights, and cultural traditions. At worst this view regards the Bible as misleading and false.

In the biblical worldview, however, God is the source of the Scriptures. He revealed Himself in words and deeds and supremely in His Son. The Bible is His written Word in which His revelation is set forth. He inspired and guided the writers to record this totally true and trustworthy revelation of Himself to humanity.

Word Study: *moved*

The word Peter used in 2 Peter 1:21 translated "moved" is *pheromenoi*. This word means "bring" or "carry." For example, Barnabas sold a field "and brought the money, and laid it at the apostles' feet" (Acts 4:37). In the passive voice, it means to be brought or carried. During the storm at sea, on the ship transporting Paul to Rome, Luke wrote that they "were driven" by the wind (Acts 27:17). In a similar way, the prophets "were moved by the Holy Ghost" (2 Pet. 1:21). It can also be translated "carried along" (NIV). The same Greek word is also found in 2 Peter 1:17 and 21a, where is can be translated "came" or "borne."

❖ Search the Scriptures

God spoke in many ways and times through the prophets, but He spoke His clearest word in His Son. The apostles as eyewitnesses were the human instruments of God in writing the New Testament. Prophets did not speak their own views, but they declared God's Word as the Holy Spirit moved them. The Focal Passage Outline points affirm that God is the source of the Bible.

The One Source of Revelation (Heb. 1:1-2)

How do these verses answer the critics who say that God is silent? How did God speak through the prophets? How did He speak in the Son? What do these two phases of revelation have in common and how are they different? What implication do these verses have on understanding the Old and New Testaments?

Hebrews 1:1-2: God, who at sundry times and in divers manners spake in time past unto the fathers by the prophets, [2]hath in these last days spoken unto us by his Son, whom he hath appointed heir of all things, by whom also he made the worlds.

Many unbelievers would agree with what a character called the Heckler in Tennessee Williams play *Sweet Bird of Youth* said: "I believe that the silence of God, the absolute speechlessness of Him is a long, long and awful thing that the whole world is lost because of. I think it's yet to be broken to any man, living or yet lived on earth—no exceptions."[1] The Heckler's anger was provoked by the pious hypocrisy of a corrupt demagogue who claimed that his political career was a response to God's call.

This is the point of view of many skeptics who claim that God— if there is a God—remains silent in the face of human suffering and injustice. This is a totally different view from the one affirmed in Hebrews 1:1-2. The main verb in verses 1-2a is **hath . . . spoken.** This verb is supported by a participle in the first part of the sentence that says that God **spake** ("spoke," NIV). Both words are forms of the word *laleo,* which means "to speak." Contrary to the claims that God is silent, these verses strongly affirm that God has not been silent.

Two phases of God's speaking are set forth by the author of Hebrews. Both stages of His speaking took written form in the Bible. Verse 1 refers to God's speaking that is now in written form in the Old Testament. Verse 2 refers to His speaking that is now in written form in the New Testament. Notice the differences in these two stages of revelation, but keep in mind that the same God was speaking in each stage.

Verse 1 is a concise summary of divine revelation in Old Testament times. God spoke **at sundry times and in divers manners** ("at many times and in various ways," NIV; "in different times and in different ways," HCSB). He spoke **in time past** ("in the past," NIV; "long ago," HCSB); that is, before the coming of Christ. He spoke **unto the fathers** ("to our forefathers," NIV); that is, to the children of Israel. He spoke **by** ("through," NIV) **the prophets.** In this context, the author of Hebrews was not limiting himself to the men who wrote the books of Prophecy in the Old Testament or even to all those who wore the title *prophet.* His statement included Abraham (Gen. 20:7), Moses (Deut. 34:10), and David (Acts 2:25,30). Thus, **the prophets** refers to all those to whom and through whom God spoke in those years, whether they were prophets, priests, kings, song writers, or wise men.

The same God spoke in the revelations of both the Old Testament and the New Testament. This is what binds the two together into what Christians define as the Holy Scriptures. However, significant differences exist between the two stages of revelation, even though each stage represents divine revelation. Verse 2a contrasts the revelation in God's Son with the revelation through the prophets, but shows a reverent respect for both.

Verse 2a stresses that the fulfillment of the earlier revelation came in God's word spoken in His **Son.** Four contrasts stand out when we compare verse 1 with verse 2a.

First, notice the contrast between **in time past** and **in these last days.** Jesus Christ divided history. The events recorded in the four Gospels marked the end of the days of promise and the beginning of the age of fulfillment. The author of Hebrews looked forward to the future coming of Christ (2:5; 9:27-28), but the decisive event was Christ's life, death, and resurrection (9:26). Christians could live in confident hope because they already had "tasted the good word of God, and the powers of the world to come" (6:5).

The second contrast is between those who received each revelation. The earlier revelation was **unto the fathers**; the latter revelation is **unto**

us. This refers to Christians. Since the completed work of Christ, believers have been privileged to live in the full noontime of the age of fulfillment.

The third contrast is between **the prophets** and the **Son.** There were many prophets, but only one Son. Verses 2b-3 contain a sevenfold exaltation to the Son. These seven descriptions show the Son's full deity and complete revelation of the Father. This description is similar to John 1:1,14. The revelation in the Son was the revelation in a human being who was also the eternal Son of God. God's clearest revelation is in the coming, ministry, teachings, death, and resurrection of Jesus Christ.

The fourth contrast is between a revelation **at sundry times and in divers manners** and the full revelation in Christ. The revelations to the prophets came at various stages in the history of God's dealings with humanity before the coming of Christ. The revelations took a variety of modes and forms. God spoke to the prophets, who delivered His words to the people. God revealed Himself in divine deliverances. He revealed Himself in miracles, visions, nature, and judgments. Sometimes God spoke in fire from heaven and sometimes in a still small voice.

The final and full revelation stands in contrast to the incomplete and diverse strands of divine revelation in the Old Testament. James T. Draper, Jr., wrote: "In the past, God spoke by the prophets in fragments, and they did not understand all of the truth of God. In the past, the prophets revealed incomplete portions of the mind of God as he revealed it to them in fragments. But now he comes to lay bare before the world the totality of his truth. Jesus Christ is the very revelation of God himself."[2] The movement from partial to full revelation is sometimes called "progressive revelation." F. F. Bruce explained, "The progression is not from the less true to the more true, from the less worthy to the more worthy, or from the less mature to the more mature" but "from promise to fulfilment."[3]

Because the Bible is the full and final revelation of God, no other book contains the true revelation of God. Other religions have their own sacred books, some of which contain some wisdom and truth—but mixed with much error. No other writing will ever be added to this final revelation.

What are the lasting lessons in Hebrews 1:1-2?

1. The revelation of God in both Testaments is inspired by God, but the Old Testament is fulfilled in the New Testament.

2. The final and superior revelation of God is in His Son.

3. Therefore, when we study the Old Testament, we need to view its ultimate meaning and application in light of the revelation in Jesus Christ.

The Superiority of the Written Word (2 Pet. 1:12-19)

*Why do Christians need reminding of their faith and way of life? Why did Peter consider his life almost over? How did he hope to continue to remind his hearers after his death? How do we know that the New Testament is true? What experience during the life of Jesus did Peter recall? How did this make **more sure** the **word of prophecy**? What did Peter mean by the **light** and the **day star**?*

2 Peter 1:12-15: Wherefore I will not be negligent to put you always in remembrance of these things, though ye know them, and be established in the present truth. [13]Yea, I think it meet, as long as I am in this tabernacle, to stir you up by putting you in remembrance; [14]knowing that shortly I must put off this my tabernacle, even as our Lord Jesus Christ hath showed me. [15]Moreover I will endeavor that ye may be able after my decease to have these things always in remembrance.

Remembrance is a key word in verses 12-15. It is found three times. Peter was reminding readers of the kinds of **things** of which he had just written in verses 1-11 and perhaps also in 1 Peter. He was not introducing something new to them, for they already were **established in the present truth.** We must not lose touch with the foundational truths of our faith and the basic characteristics of Christian living. This is one reason that the word *remember* is common in both the Old and New Testaments.

One reason for Peter's sense of urgency was that he felt that his life was about to end. **Tabernacle** here means "tent" (NIV), or more clearly, "the tent of this body" (NIV). Why did Peter feel that death was near? He mentioned that **our Lord Jesus Christ** had **showed** him this fact. Persecution of Christians was increasing, and Peter expected to be killed. This realization led Peter to make two commitments. First, he was committed to remind his readers of these things as long as he was alive. Second, he intended to continue to remind them after his death.

Christians leave the time of their death in the hands of God. Our awareness of life's shortness and uncertainty makes us realize that we need to work while it is day, for the night comes when no one can work. Older believers sometimes feel that their lives are almost over and, therefore, there is nothing left for them to do. This is not true. As long as we live, we should do what we can for as long as we can and as well as we can.

But how did Peter expect to continue to remind his readers after he was dead? The most likely answer is that he hoped that his writings would help do this. We are not told whether the apostles knew they were writing what became part of the inspired Scriptures of the new covenant. Yet in 2 Peter 3:15-16 Peter referred to Paul's letters as taking their place among the other Scriptures. Apparently the churches saved letters from the apostles and shared them with other churches. Peter wrote in the hope that God would continue to use his words to remind his readers of the basic truths of the faith.

Peter's words help us understand some of the process by which God inspired the apostles to write. The apostles wrote letters to address specific needs in their day as they were led by the Spirit to interpret and apply the mind of Christ to a variety of issues.

2 Peter 1:16-18: For we have not followed cunningly devised fables, when we made known unto you the power and coming of our Lord Jesus Christ, but were eyewitnesses of his majesty. [17]For he received from God the Father honor and glory, when there came such a voice to him from the excellent glory, This is my beloved Son, in whom I am well-pleased. [18]And this voice which came from heaven we heard, when we were with him in the holy mount.

Peter denied that what he said and wrote were **cunningly devised fables** ("cleverly invented stories," NIV). "The word **fables** *(muthoi)* carried a disparaging flavour in the religious language of the time; it stood for mythical stories about gods, the creation of the world, miraculous happenings, etc."[4] Peter strongly denied that the apostles were speaking such obviously false teachings **when** they **made known unto** their hearers **the power and coming of our Lord Jesus Christ.** They spoke and wrote as **eyewitnesses of his majesty.**

How do we know the New Testament contains the truth about Jesus? We know because the apostles were **eyewitnesses** of the things of which they spoke and wrote. Peter gave an example of one of the events from the life of Jesus that he had witnessed. Verses 17-18 refer to the transfiguration of Jesus, which Peter, James, and John had seen. Three of the Gospels tell what happened (Matt. 17:1-13; Mark 9:1-13; Luke 9:28-36). Shortly after Peter's confession at Caesarea Philippi and Jesus' first prediction of His death and resurrection, Jesus took these three disciples onto the mountain where He was transfigured with the brightness of the glory of God. During that experience, the awed disciples **heard** the **voice which came from heaven.** As God had done at the baptism of Jesus, He said of Jesus, **This is my beloved Son, in whom I am well-pleased.** In saying this, God made clear that Jesus was His Son who would save a lost world by His suffering and death. The heavenly voice combined one of the kingly passages (Ps. 2:7) with one of the Servant passages (Isa. 42:1). The transfiguration also foreshadowed the future glory of Jesus. This was seen in His resurrection, and it will be seen in His future coming.

Peter was a witness of the transfiguration, of the resurrection, and of the Lord's promised return. In his writings he emphasized the redeeming death of Jesus and our living hope based on His resurrection from the dead (1 Pet. 1:3-5,18-19). He also stressed the importance of being ready for Christ's future coming. Apparently this coming was in his mind when he wrote these verses. In other words, the transfiguration, with its revelation of the glory of God, points toward the ultimate fulfillment of His saving purpose in the future coming. The word **coming** in verse 16 is *parousia,* which can mean "presence" or "coming." When used to mean "coming," the New Testament uses it to refer to Christ's future coming.

The point of verses 16-18 to this study on the Bible is that people who were eyewitnesses of God's revelation wrote the Bible. The New Testament consists of the inspired words of those who were eyewitnesses of what they wrote. We know the Bible is true for two basic reasons. For one thing, the writers were inspired by God's Spirit to write the truth. Second, they wrote as people who had witnessed God's revelation. The Old Testament is the prophetic witness to the words and acts of God in their day. The New Testament is the inspired witness of the apostles to what they had seen and heard. We have the testimony of the original apostles whom Jesus called, trained, and commissioned as His witnesses. This final revelation is the New Testament.

2 Peter 1:19: **We have also a more sure word of prophecy; whereunto ye do well that ye take heed, as unto a light that shineth in a dark place, until the day dawn, and the day star arise in your hearts.**

This verse is a transition from verses 16-18 to verses 20-21. **Word of prophecy** refers to the prophetic word of God through Old Testament prophets. As was true in Hebrews 1:1, this referred not just to the writing prophets but also to all the Old Testament. The word for **sure** appeared in verse 10. *Bebaiosis* is a legal term for a guarantee for a buyer that what he purchased was his. **More sure** is *bebaioteron.* In what sense did the transfiguration make the Old Testament prophets **more sure**?

William Barclay paraphrased two views. One says: "In prophecy we have an even surer guarantee, that is, of the Second Coming." This view puts the words of the prophets in a higher position than the eye-witnesses' personal experience on the Mount of Transfiguration. A more likely view, Barclay believed, is "What we saw on the Mount of Transfiguration makes it even more certain that what is foretold in the prophets about the Second Coming must be true." Barclay wrote, "However we take this, the meaning of it is that the glory of Jesus on the mountain top and the visions of the prophets combine to make certain the Second Coming is a living reality which all men must expect, and for which all men must prepare."[5]

Peter challenged his readers to **take heed** ("pay attention," NIV). Then he described the future coming in several ways. It will be like **a light that shineth in a dark place.** He connected this with the **dawn** of a new **day** when the night becomes dawn. These pictures are easy to understand, but the last part of verse 19 has several possible inter-pretations. What is **the day star** and how will it **arise in** human **hearts**? **Day star** translates a word found only here in biblical Greek. *Phosphoros* literally means "light-bringer." It is often translated as "morning star" (NIV), but others see it as the sun rising on a new day. Some Bible students feel that the "light-bringer" refers to the Son of God Himself. They point to the Old Testament prophecy of the coming of a star (Num. 24:17), to New Testament references to Him as "the dayspring from on high" (Luke 1:78) and "the bright and morning star" (Rev. 22:16).

What are the lasting truths of 2 Peter 1:12-19?

1. Christians need to be reminded and to remind one another of the basics of their faith.

2. The Bible is the primary means of reminding us of the truth.

3. The Bible is not myths and fables but inspired words of those who experienced unique revelation from God.

4. The apostles were eyewitnesses of events such as the transfiguration of Jesus.

5. The prophets and events such as the transfiguration point to the future coming of Christ.

The Divine Origin of the Scriptures (2 Pet. 1:20-21)

Does verse 20 refer to **interpretation** *by the prophets or by individuals? Why is it important to affirm that the Scriptures were not* *by the will of man? Why is it important to affirm that the Scriptures are from God? How do the Scriptures combine the divine and the human? What is the role of the Holy Spirit? What implications for personal Bible use come from the truth of verse 21?*

2 Peter 1:20-21: Knowing this first, that no prophecy of the scripture is of any private interpretation. [21]For the prophecy came not in old time by the will of man: but holy men of God spake as they were moved by the Holy Ghost [Spirit].

Some Bible students think that the meaning of verse 20 applies to how individuals interpret the Bible. Others believe that the meaning applies to how the prophets interpreted the Scriptures they wrote. The key word **private** in the Greek text is *idias,* which means "their own." The question is, who is being referred to—the writers or the readers of the Bible? *The New Revised Standard Version* reads, "No prophecy of scripture is a matter of one's own interpretation." The *New International Version* assumes that Peter meant the prophets: "No prophecy of Scripture came about by the prophet's own interpretation."

If verse 20 refers to the prophet's own interpretation, verse 20 makes one of the same points as verse 21. The point is that prophets did not speak and write **by the will of man.** Instead, **they were moved by the Holy Ghost** ("they were carried along by the Holy Spirit," NIV; "they were . . . impelled by the Holy Spirit," NEB). Just as a wind moves a sailboat, so did the Spirit move the prophets as they spoke and wrote God's Word. This is the only mention of the Holy Spirit in 2 Peter, but what a significant message!

This is a strong affirmation that the Scriptures had their origin in God. Yet the verse also affirms that God used human beings to write the books of the Bible. Many people over many years were the writers of Scripture. Each wrote in his own style. However, because God is the source of the writing, the Bible has a remarkable unity.

Even if verse 20 refers to prophets, not to each interpreter, verse 21 has strong implications for each person who seeks to understand God's Word. The same Spirit who inspired the writers is with readers to illumine their minds and move in their hearts. Thus we must come to the Bible with reverence and faith.

What are the lasting truths of verses 20-21?

1. The writers of the Bible did not write based on their own intentions or interests.

2. Writers of God's Word wrote as they were carried along by the Holy Spirit.

3. The writers were humans who each wrote in his own style, but God's Spirit worked within each writer so that the Bible has one true source—God.

4. The same Spirit who inspired the Bible's writers will also illumine those who read the Bible.

❖ *Spiritual Transformations*

God has spoken in both the Old and New Testaments. Jesus, the Son of God, is the fulfillment of the promises of the old covenant and the supreme and final revelation of God. The Bible is the inspired testimony of the prophets and the apostles to God's revelation. The Bible's writers did not write from theirs or any other human's ideas and reflections. The Holy Spirit inspired them with the result that the combination of these 66 books constitutes the written Word of God.

Christians need to have strong faith in the divine origin of the Bible. In every way possible we should affirm the Bible as the true and trustworthy Word of God. This can be done in words and in actions. People who truly believe that God's message for each of them is in the Bible will saturate their minds and hearts with the message of the Bible. They will take advantage of every opportunity to affirm the Bible by what they say and what they do.

What place does the Bible have in your life? _____

How often do you read the Bible? _____

How often do you study the Bible seriously? _____

How often do you act based on Bible teachings? _____

Prayer of Commitment: Dear God, I thank You for Your Word. Help me to live and to speak in accordance with Your revelation. Amen.

[1]Tennessee Williams, *Sweet Bird of Youth* [New York: Two Rivers Enterprises, Inc., 1959], 105.

[2]James T. Draper, Jr., *Hebrews: The Life that Pleases God* [Wheaton, Illinois: Tyndale House Publishers, Inc., 1976], 13.

[3]F. F. Bruce, *The Epistle to the Hebrews,* in The New International Commentary on the New Testament [Grand Rapids: William B. Eerdmans Publishing Company, 1964], 2.

[4]J. N. D. Kelly, *A Commentary on the Epistles of Peter and of Jude,* in the Harper New Testament Commentaries [Peabody, Massachusetts: Hendrickson Publishers, 1988], 316.

[5]William Barclay, *The Letters of James and Peter,* in The Daily Study Bible, 2nd ed., [Philadelphia: The Westminster Press, 1960], 367-368.

THE BIBLE: ITS VALUE

Background Passage: Psalm 119:9-16; Jeremiah 36:1-32
Focal Passage: Psalm 119:9-16; Jeremiah 36:2-3,21-24,27-28
Key Verse: Psalm 119:16

❖ *Significance of the Lesson*

• The *Theme* of this lesson is that our attitude should reflect that the Bible is a perfect treasure of divine instruction.
• The *Life Question* this lesson seeks to address is, Why should I value the Bible?
• The *Biblical Truth* is that the Bible is a perfect treasure of divine instruction.
• The *Life Impact* is to help you treasure the Bible.

How Valuable Is the Bible?

In secular worldviews, the Bible is dismissed as irrelevant. Many simply ignore the Bible, but some attack it as useless and out-of-date.

In the biblical worldview, the Bible is the Word of God, which delivers the message of God's grace or judgment. It is a perfect treasure of divine instruction.

Word Study: *testimonies*

The Hebrew word translated "testimonies" in Psalm 119:14 is *'edut*. It also can be translated "statutes" (NIV). This is one of 10 words used in Psalm 119 to refer to the written Word of God. Derek Kidner wrote of this word: "Israel was told to place the book of the law beside the ark of the covenant 'that it may be there for a witness (*'ed*) against you' (Dt. 31:26). The outspokenness of Scripture, with its high standards and frank warnings (*e.g.* Dt. 8:19, using this root), is implied in this expression, but so too is its dependability, as the word of the 'faithful and true witness'. Therefore 'thy testimonies are my delight' (v. 24)."[1]

❖ *Search the Scriptures*

Psalm 119 focuses on the Word of God as a treasure. Verses 9-11 emphasize the power of the Word to cleanse and to keep life morally clean. Verses 12-16 show joy and delight in the Word. Jeremiah 36: 2-3 shows that the Word of God is intended to lead sinners to repent. Jeremiah 36:21-24 gives an example of someone seeking to destroy the Word. Jeremiah 36:27-28 reveals God's command for the destroyed parts of the Word of God to be rewritten.

The four outline points are characteristics of God's Word that lead us to value it.

A Purifying Treasure (Ps. 119:9-11)

*Why were young men singled out? How does the word **cleanse**? Why is wandering a danger? How is God's Word **hid** in your heart? How does this keep you from sin?*

Psalm 119:9-11: Wherewithal shall a young man cleanse his way? By taking heed thereto according to thy word. ¹⁰With my whole heart have I sought thee: O let me not wander from thy commandments. ¹¹Thy word have I hid in mine heart, that I might not sin against thee.

The Word of God is the basis for the moral foundation of society and of each person. Since all have sinned, the Word first convicts us of our sins. Then it points us to God, who offers to forgive those who repent. **Cleanse** in verse 9 seems to be used here not only of being cleansed but also of being kept cleansed, as the *New International Version* reads, "How can a young man keep his way pure?" The focus is on young men because they seem to have the greatest struggle remaining pure. Too many have been taught that they are expected to sow their wild oats, but they have not been warned that they will reap what they sow.

The last part of verse 9 answers the question of the first part. Anyone—young or old, man or woman—can remain pure by **taking heed** ("living," NIV; "keeping," NASB; "guarding," NRSV) **thereto according to** God's **word.** This involves giving attention to knowing the Word and living according to its teachings.

The psalmist testified that he had **sought** the Lord **with** his **whole heart.** The Bible defines true devotion only in terms of seeking God with all our hearts. To fail to give wholehearted devotion to God is to risk the danger against which the last part of verse 10 warns. The psalmist prayed, **Let me not wander from thy commandments. Wander** reminds us of sheep that have gone astray. All of us had gone astray before God's grace overtook us. The danger of wandering continues even after conversion.

> O to grace how great a debtor
>> Daily I'm constrained to be!
> Let Thy grace, Lord, like a fetter,
>> Bind my wand'ring heart to Thee:
> Prone to wander, Lord, I feel it,
>> Prone to leave the God I love;
> Here's my heart, Lord, take and seal it,
>> Seal it for Thy courts above.[2]

The psalmist sought to avoid wandering by hiding God's Word **in his heart.** The purpose was that he **might not sin against** God. Hiding God's Word in your heart involves knowing the Word, memorizing key verses, and applying the Word to times when you need to hear and obey God's Word. When Jesus was tempted, He quoted Scripture to ward off the tempter's subtle lies. When the devil quoted Scripture, Jesus recognized the false application being made of it; and Jesus countered with a verse that did apply to His situation (Matt. 4:1-11; Luke 4:1-13).

Someone has said, "This book will keep you from sin, and sin will keep you from this book." When people have lived according to the Bible, righteousness, peace, and joy have reigned. When people have rejected or wandered from the Bible, sin, strife, and misery have followed.

Although the Bible is still a best seller and although we have enough translations in English for anyone to understand the message, we live in a time when many people reject the Bible, do not know it, or disobey it. Amos 8:11-12 warns of a time when there would be a famine of the Word of God. Many people already live in such a time in their own lives. No wonder that sins of all kinds are either committed or condoned. We live in a time like that described in Isaiah 5:20: "Woe unto them that call evil good, and good evil; that put darkness for light, and light for darkness; that put bitter for sweet, and sweet for bitter!"

What are the lasting lessons of Psalm 119:9-11?

1. The Word of God is valuable in convicting of sin, leading to repentance, helping to live a good life, and overcoming temptations.

2. For this to be true, people must seek God with all their hearts, hide His Word in their hearts, and live according to His Word.

3. When people know and obey the Bible, life is the best it can be; when people are ignorant of or disobedient to God's Word, life turns sour.

A Delightful Treasure (Ps. 119:12-16)

Why do some people find joy and delight in the Bible and other people find it boring? Why is the Bible better that great riches? What are the conditions for seeing the Bible as a treasure? How do people neglect the Bible?

Psalm 119:12-16: Blessed art thou, O LORD: teach me thy statutes. [13]With my lips have I declared all the judgments of thy mouth. [14]I have rejoiced in the way of thy testimonies, as much as in all riches. [15]I will meditate in thy precepts, and have respect unto thy ways. [16]I will delight myself in thy statutes: I will not forget thy word.

The key words in these verses are **rejoiced** and **delight.** Derek Kidner wrote of Psalm 119: "A persistent theme is the *delight* these sayings bring. The first references to this, in verses 14 and 16, set the tone of much that will follow. . . . This is not merely a scholar's pleasure (though it has this aspect, v. 97) but a disciple's, whose joy is in obedience."[3]

These themes of joy and delight continue throughout this song of praise to God for His Word. The length and other distinctives of the psalm testify to the reality of the psalmist's joy. Only such a person would have written a song of 176 lines, with 22 verses of 8 lines each, and with each of the lines in a stanza beginning with the same letter of the alphabet.

The writer **rejoiced in the way of** God's **testimonies, as much as in all riches.** This theme of the value of the Word is found throughout the psalm (see vv. 72,111,127,162). How much is your Bible worth to you? In terms of financial cost of buying a copy of a Bible, you can buy one for just a few dollars. Groups such as the Gideons give Bibles away. You can buy a fairly expensive Bible if you choose. However, the real value of a Bible that is used is beyond any monetary value. This assumes, of course, that you have made the Word of God prominent in your study and in your actions. Then it is priceless.

During the second World War, a Marine chaplain told of his ministry among the men of his unit. After one of the bloody battles in New Guinea, the chaplain was walking through the battle area. He came upon a place where a Marine died. Scattered about was the gear of a Marine: his pack, machete, ammunition, food, and writing pad. The chaplain also noticed something else that particularly moved him. He wrote: "As I poked around those forlorn remnants of this unknown Marine, I uncovered near his pack a well-worn New Testament half hidden in the mud. I rejoiced. It was a good sign! His physical life had been sacrificed on the heartless altar of war, sacrificed on Christmas day, but I like to believe that he knew the secret of peace and eternal life through Jesus Christ the Lord. Those who are not Christians do not read their Testaments until they are well-worn and much-thumbed."[4]

The value we place on the Bible is not measured by the cost of the copy we have but by the use we make of it. In the case of the psalmist, he showed how he valued this treasure by how he praised the Lord (v. 12a), by his desire to be taught more of the Word (v. 12b), and by his testimonies of the Word (vv. 13-14).

Just as verse 10 was a prayer to be kept from wandering from the Word, so verse 16 ended with a commitment: **I will not forget** ("neglect," NIV) **thy word.** Many people never open a Bible. Even some church members seldom open their Bibles. They may own an expensive family Bible, which they bring out and dust off when the pastor visits in their home, but it is neglected most of the time. Let each of us join the psalmist in this commitment not to neglect the Word of God. Let us read it, study it, meditate on it, listen to it preached and taught, and practice what it teaches.

What are the lasting lessons of Psalm 119:12-16?

1. The Bible is a priceless gift from God.
2. Christians should find joy and delight in the Word of God.
3. This joy should be seen in how we receive and respond to the Bible.

A Purposeful Treasure (Jer. 36:2-3)

What is the significance of Jeremiah 36? What writing material was used in Jeremiah's day? How did the spoken message of God through Jeremiah take written form? What did God tell Jeremiah to do with the written messages? What insight does this chapter give us about how the Word of God took written form?

Jeremiah 36:2-3: **Take thee a roll of a book, and write therein all the words that I have spoken unto thee against Israel, and against Judah, and against all the nations, from the day I spake unto thee, from the days of Josiah, even unto this day. ³It may be that the house of Judah will hear all the evil which I purpose to do unto them; that they may return every man from his evil way; that I may forgive their iniquity and their sin.**

This is a significant chapter in the Book of Jeremiah. For one thing, "it is the only passage in the OT that shows one way a prophet's oral messages reached their written form."[5] God told Jeremiah to make a written copy of all the words of God that the prophet had spoken since the beginning of his ministry. Jeremiah had begun his ministry in 627 B.C. during the reign of Josiah. This chapter took place in the fourth year of Jehoiakim [jih-HOY-uh-kim] (605 B.C.). Jeremiah was a prophet primarily to **Judah,** but he also had spoken words concerning **all the nations.**

A roll of a book literally means "a scroll of a writing." Books as we know them were not used until later. "Scrolls were made of papyrus or leather sheets sewn together with the writing placed in columns. Jeremiah's scroll probably was written on papyrus since it would have been easier to burn than leather (see 36:23). A typical scroll measured thirty feet by ten inches. It was wrapped on wooden rollers and rolled from one side to the other as it was read."[6] More important than the writing material was the fact that God told Jeremiah to put the spoken words into writing. Jeremiah did not write the words on the scroll. He enlisted Baruch [BEHR-uhk] to write as Jeremiah dictated to him (v. 4).

The Bible does not tell us much about the process in which the books of the Bible were written. This is thus especially valuable since it gives a kind of model for how it was done. First of all, God revealed Himself. He did this sometimes in words, as in the case of Jeremiah, and sometimes in some other way. For example, He revealed Himself to John in visions and told him to write what he saw (Rev. 1:11,19). Whatever the mode of revelation, God revealed Himself to certain people. Then He led those whom He had chosen to put the revelation into written form. During the writing, His Spirit inspired the writers so that the written product was the Word of God. In some cases the human author had someone else to actually put the words on the writing surface. Jeremiah used Baruch. In writing Romans, Paul used Tertius (Rom. 16:22). God oversaw the entire process so that His revelation was accurate and true.

We cannot tell exactly what parts of the present Book of Jeremiah were in that first copy. The chapters in the book are not in chronological order. Also verse 32 tells us that additional material was included in the second copy. The first copy must have been short enough to be read to three different groups on one day (vv. 8,15,21). But it must have contained enough of the prophet's messages of coming judgment to arouse the hostility of the king. The immediate purpose of the written book was to bring together all the messages of the Lord through Jeremiah so that the hearers would hear **all the evil** that the Lord would send unless they repented. An unspoken reason was that the words of God spoken through Jeremiah could reach more people in his own day and beyond his day. The prophet was mortal, and the written words could long outlast him.

The Lord's purpose was **that they may return every man from his evil way.** When this happened, God would **forgive their iniquity and their sin.** Although the fate of the nation had been sealed by the weight of sins of generations, including that generation, God offered forgiveness to all who turned from sin and turned to the Lord. Jeremiah prophesied of a new covenant in which forgiveness was a key feature (see 31:31-34). Yet even in Old Testament times, God called sinners to repent and be forgiven (Ex. 34:6-7; Isa. 1:18; 55:6-7).

What are the lasting lessons of Jeremiah 36:2-3?

1. God revealed Himself and led prophets and apostles to write accurately what He revealed.

2. The written Word of God enables each generation to read God's revelation.

3. A merciful God offers forgiveness to those who turn from sin to Him.

An Indestructible Treasure (Jer. 36:21-24,27-28)

How did Jehoiakim come to hear the words of Jeremiah? How did he respond? How can his reaction be explained? What did God command Jeremiah to do? Why is the Word of God indestructible?

Jeremiah 36:21-24: So the king sent Jehudi to fetch the roll: and he took it out of Elishama the scribe's chamber. And Jehudi read it in the ears of the king, and in the ears of all the princes which stood beside the king. [22]Now the king sat in the winterhouse in the ninth month: and there was a fire on the hearth burning before him.

²³**And it came to pass, that when Jehudi had read three or four leaves, he cut it with the penknife, and cast it into the fire that was on the hearth, until all the roll was consumed in the fire that was on the hearth.** ²⁴**Yet they were not afraid, nor rent their garments, neither the king, nor any of his servants that heard all these words.**

When the officials reported the existence of the scroll to the king, he asked that it be read to him. **Jehudi** [jih-HYOO-digh], one of the officials, **read** the scroll to **the king** and to **all the princes which stood beside the king.**

They were **in the winterhouse.** This was not necessarily a separate house in a warmer part of the land. It was the first floor of the palace, which could be heated better than the second floor, and was used in warmer weather. Some believe the words **there was a fire on the hearth burning before him** indicate that the fire was in a movable "firepot" (NIV). Either way, the king was close enough to the fire to put things in it.

As Jehudi **read three or four leaves** ("columns," NIV), the king **cut it with the penknife, and cast it into the fire.** This deadly process continued "until the entire scroll was burned in the fire" (NIV). There is no record of any outward emotion by the king, but his insides must have seethed with hostility. The text states, "The king and all his attendants who heard all these words showed no fear, nor did they tear their clothes" (NIV). In other words, no one showed any sense of godly sorrow for their sins. Everything was done with cold calculation.

What a contrast Jehoiakim was to his father Josiah. During Josiah's reign the scroll of the law was found in the temple. When the young king heard the words read, he tore his clothes (2 Kings 22:11). Then he set out to uproot idolatry and led in a national spiritual revival. Josiah's son had no such response. In fact, his was the opposite response. He ordered the arrest of Jeremiah and Baruch (Jer. 36:26).

Jeremiah 36:27-28: **Then the word of the LORD came to Jeremiah, after that the king had burned the roll, and the words which Baruch wrote at the mouth of Jeremiah, saying,** ²⁸**Take thee again another roll, and write in it all the former words that were in the first roll, which Jehoiakim the king of Judah hath burned.**

God hid Jeremiah and Baruch. He told Jeremiah to take another scroll and **write in it all the former words that were in the first roll** ("scroll," NIV). God also told Jeremiah to tell Jehoiakim of the judgment coming on him and the nation. Jeremiah obeyed the Lord and again enlisted Baruch as the scribe. "As Jeremiah dictated, Baruch wrote on it all the words of the scroll that Jehoiakim the king of Judah had burned in the fire. And many similar words were added to them" (v. 32, NIV). God's Spirit inspired Jeremiah to recall the words from the first scroll and led him to add other messages.

This is one of the best biblical examples of a vicious attempt to destroy the written Word of God and of the indestructible nature of the Word. Throughout history many people have rejected the message of the Bible, and some of them have launched vicious attacks on it. All too often these attacks have attempted to destroy the Bible and those who spread it to others. The enemies of the Bible have sometimes burned copies of the Bible and even those who promoted it, but they have not stopped the distribution of the written Word of God.

After the invention of the printing press, Bible believers were able to print more copies of the Holy Scriptures. Herschel H. Hobbs told of the work of William Tyndale, whose story is parallel to Jeremiah 36 in several ways. Tyndale translated the New Testament into English, using Greek manuscripts. Opposition to him and his Bible forced him to flee from England to the continent, where he continued his work. "It is said that he finished setting his type late one afternoon. During the night vandals destroyed the type. But patiently he resumed the task, finishing it by the end of 1525. The next year he smuggled Bibles into England in sacks of flour. They were joyfully received by the people, but the bishops sent agents to buy and destroy them. However, the Bibles continued to come until the country was flooded with copies of the New Testament in English. As a result of this work, Tyndale was arrested and on October 6, 1536, was strangled and burned. His dying prayer was, 'Lord, open the King of England's eyes.' His prayer was answered with the publication of the King James Version of the Bible in 1611."[7]

I paused last eve beside the blacksmith's door,
    And heard the anvil ring, the vesper's chime,
And looking in I saw upon the floor
    Old hammers, worn with beating years of time.
"How many anvils have you had?" said I,
    "To wear and batter all these hammers so?"
"Just one," he answered. Then with twinkling eye:
    "The anvil wears the hammers out, you know."
And so, I thought, the anvil of God's Word
    For ages skeptics' blows have beat upon,

> But though the noise of falling blows was heard
> The anvil is unchanged; the hammers gone.[8]

What are the lasting lessons of Jeremiah 36:21-24,27-28?

1. Many people have sought to destroy the Bible.
2. The Word of God continues to exert its power.

❖ *Spiritual Transformations*

The Word of God is a precious treasure for several reasons. It enables people to be forgiven and to live pure lives. Believers find joy in it. God led in the writing of the Bible in order, first of all, to call people to repent and be forgiven of their sins. Although enemies have sought to destroy the Bible, it is indestructible.

This lesson is about valuing the Bible as a treasure. How do people show how little or how much value they place on the Bible? One way is how much they read and study it. The other key test is how closely to its teachings they live.

How could you give more time and effort to reading and studying the Bible? _____

How could you live more diligently according to the Bible's teachings? _____

Prayer of Commitment: Lord, thank You for Your precious Word. Help me to grow in understanding and in obedience based on Your Word. Amen.

---

[1]Kidner, *Psalms 73–150*, 418.

[2]Robert Robinson, "Come, Thou Fount of Every Blessing," No. 15, *The Baptist Hymnal*, 1991.

[3]Kidner, *Psalms 73–150*, 420.

[4]Arthur F. Glasser, *And Some Believed* [Chicago: Moody Press, 1946], 156.

[5]F. B. Huey, Jr., "Jeremiah, Lamentations," in *The New American Commentary*, vol. 16 [Nashville: Broadman Press, 1993], 318.

[6]Huey, "Jeremiah, Lamentations," NAC, 319.

[7]Herschel H. Hobbs, *Fundamentals of Our Faith* [Nashville: Broadman Press, 1960], 6.

[8]John Clifford, "God's Word," in *Masterpieces of Religious Verse*, 493.

THE BIBLE: ITS PURPOSE

Bible Passage: Psalm 19:7-14; 2 Timothy 3:14-17
Key Verses: 2 Timothy 3:16-17

❖ *Significance of the Lesson*

• The *Theme* of this lesson is that the Bible tells us how to live. It is the supreme standard by which all human conduct, creeds, and religious opinions should be tried.
• The *Life Question* addressed by this lesson is, Why should I study the Bible?
• The *Biblical Truth* is that the Bible is God's supreme standard for salvation and Christian living.
• The *Life Impact* is to help you live by biblical standards.

Standards

In the secular worldview, people turn to various sources for guidance in their beliefs and behavior, including society about them and human heroes of the past. Others are convinced that no absolute standards exist.

In the biblical worldview, the Bible is the supreme standard by which all human conduct, creeds, and religious opinions are to be tried.

Word Study: *instruction in righteousness*

The Greek for the phrase **instruction in righteousness** in 2 Timothy 3:16 is *paideian ten en dikaiosune. Paidion* is the word for "child." The verb *paideuo* means to "bring up," "instruct," or "train." The noun *paideia* means "upbringing," "training," "instruction," or "discipline." Although the verb is used of training children in Ephesians 6:4, the verb and the noun are also used of instruction of people of all ages, as it is used in this passage in 2 Timothy. This instruction assumes that believers are right with God and thus can be trained to live a righteous life by the power of God's Spirit.

❖ *Search the Scriptures*

The law or Word of God is perfect, as is the Lord who stands behind it. It convicts of sin and leads us to seek forgiveness and moral strength from the Lord. The Holy Scriptures have two main purposes. First, they seek to lead to salvation in Christ. Then these inspired Scriptures become the standard and source for doctrine and godly living.

The four outline points describe the characteristics of the Bible as the standard by which believers are to live, thus fulfilling the Life Impact.

Perfect Standard (Ps. 19:7-11)

*What is the significance of the repeated use of **the Lord**? What words describe **the law of the Lord**? What words describe its characteristics? What words describe its benefits? What two things is it compared to? What does it mean to live by the Word of God as our standard?*

Psalm 19:7-9: The law of the Lord is perfect, converting the soul: the testimony of the Lord is sure, making wise the simple. ⁸The statutes of the Lord are right, rejoicing the heart: the commandment of the Lord is pure, enlightening the eyes. ⁹The fear of the Lord is clean, enduring forever: the judgments of the Lord are true and righteous altogether.

Four things about **the law of the Lord** are in verses 7-9. These are found in six statements. First, let me call attention to the name of God. Verses 1-6 use the general name for God—*Elohim.* This is appropriate because these verses are about the revelation of God the Creator in His creation. **The Lord** is the personal name of the God who made the covenant with Israel—*Yahweh.* The words **of the Lord** are in each of the six statements and the word **Lord** is also in verse 14. Elmer A. Leslie noted, "The sevenfold appearance of the name of Israel's God (i.e., Yahweh) . . . is intended to suggest the perfection of His revelation."[1] This repetition of the words **of the Lord** also shows that **the law** is from God and reflects the Lord's character. What He expects of His people is that they be like Him.

The second thing about the six statements is the use of six different words for **the law.** Four of these are basically synonyms for **the law.** Just as in Psalm 119, several different words are used for the same reality. **The law** can also be called **testimony . . . statutes . . . commandment . . . judgments.** The use of **fear** in verse 9 is more of a response to the law than another name for it. Actually **the law** or *Torah* can refer to one law, the Ten Commandments, to all the laws given to Israel, to the first five books of the Bible, or to the entire Bible.

The third feature of the six statements is the use of six different words that describe this Word of God. It is **perfect,** just as is the God who inspired it. It is **sure** in the sense of being completely "trustworthy" (NIV). It is **right** because it shows us the right way to live. It is **pure** in the sense of being "radiant" (NIV). It is **clean** in the sense of containing nothing unclean. It is **true** in every way and in every part.

The fourth feature of the statements in verses 7-9 is the list of six benefits from being in the Word of God. **Converting the soul** can refer to initial conversion or to "reviving" (NIV) or "restoring the soul" (NASB). **Making wise the simple** promises that the Word will impart to the humble wisdom to live in God's will and way. **Rejoicing the heart** is one benefit of living the **right** way according to God's Word. **Enlightening the eyes** means providing the insight needed to see reality through the eyes of faith. These benefits are **enduring forever.** Indeed, **the judgments of the LORD are true and righteous altogether.**

Psalm 19:10-11: **More to be desired are they than gold, yea, than much fine gold: sweeter also than honey and the honeycomb. [11]Moreover by them is thy servant warned: and in keeping of them there is great reward.**

Verse 10 uses two comparisons to show the surpassing worth of the Word of God. The word for **gold** refers to pure gold. Throughout the centuries gold has been considered among the most valuable possessions. The teachings of the Scriptures are more precious **than gold.** Among the most desirable foods in that day was **honey.** The Scriptures are **sweeter also than honey and the honeycomb.**

Verse 11 begins a prayer to the Lord. Verses 7-10 were about God's Word. Then the psalmist addressed God directly about His Word. He humbly referred to himself as the Lord's **servant.** Another benefit of the Word of God is that believers are **warned** of dangers to avoid. We should thank God for the warnings of His Word. The positive side of verse 11 is the grateful acknowledgment to God of the **great reward** that comes from **keeping** the teachings of His Word.

Verses 7-11 emphasize that the Bible is a perfect standard for our beliefs and practices. The Word of God is like a yardstick. Whenever we dare to lay our lives down beside this divine yardstick, we see our sins and shortcomings. With God's help we can seek to better measure up according to His standard. This is one reason we never graduate from Sunday School. Those who regularly see themselves according to God's standard seek His forgiveness and power to live in His way. Those who don't measure their lives by God's standard use some human standard, which is often contrary to God's standard.

A poll on morality found that 58 percent of Americans believe it is all right for an unmarried couple to live together. The same poll showed that 37 percent think profanity is acceptable. Although almost 75 percent said they are concerned about the moral condition of our nation, 44 percent said they base their moral decisions on what gives them the most satisfying and pleasing results. Only about 25 percent said their moral decisions are based on religious principles and biblical teachings.[2] No wonder our nation's moral condition is deplorable. People either do not know what the Bible teaches or they know but reject its standards in favor of doing what feels right to them at the time. This is a formula for moral disaster. The only hope for change is to adopt the Bible as the perfect standard for living.

What are the lasting lessons in Psalm 19:7-11?

1. The Word of the Lord is perfect.
2. God's Word converts, renews, reveals, enlightens, and endures.
3. God's Word is more valuable than gold.
4. The Word of God is the standard by which believers seek to live.

Standard to Reveal Sin (Ps. 19:12-14)

What two categories of sin are mentioned in these verses? What prayer is prayed about each kind of sin? With what prayer does the psalm close?

Psalm 19:12-13: Who can understand his errors? Cleanse thou me from secret faults. [13]Keep back thy servant also from presumptuous sins; let them not have dominion over me: then shall I be upright, and I shall be innocent from the great transgression.

Two categories of sins are mentioned in verses 12-13. Each one is described in two ways. The first category is in verse 12. **Errors** are unintentional sins. Sometimes the sinner is not even aware of them. Thus the psalmist asked, **Who can understand** ("discern," NIV) **his errors?** "No one can discern his faults, on account of the heart of man being unfathomable and on account of the disguise, oftentimes so plausible, and the subtlety of sin."[3] Only God can enable us to see such sins.

These sins are also called **secret** ("hidden," NIV) **faults.** The psalmist asked that the Lord would **cleanse** ("forgive," NIV) him of these sins. Thus he first wanted God to show him these sins; then he prayed that God would forgive these sins. Through His Word is often the way God gives discernment of these sins and points us to the forgiveness He offers.

The other category of sins is more serious. These **presumptuous sins** are intentional "willful sins" (NIV). These are also called the **great transgression.** These are insolent sins of deliberate rebellion against God. The psalmist prayed that the Lord would **keep** him from such terrible sins. Only in this way would he be **upright** ("blameless," NIV) and **innocent** of such sins. The danger of such sins is that they tend to **have dominion over** the sinner. God warned Cain that his sin lurked at his door threatening to rule over him. He warned Cain to deal with it before it ruined him (Gen. 4:6-7). Such sins threaten all of us at some time. Only God's enlightenment through His Word can convict us of these sins and keep us from becoming enslaved by them.

***Psalm 19:14:* Let the words of my mouth, and the meditation of my heart, be acceptable in thy sight, O LORD, my strength, and my redeemer.**

"The psalmist brings his hymn to a close in one of the classic prayers of the Psalter. He uses a term familiar in the priestly ritual, the word 'acceptable.' To be made acceptable to God, he is told by his law that he must bring the properly prescribed offering (Lev. 1:3), which will then be acceptable, pleasing unto God (Isa. 56:7). So the psalmist lifts up to God, his Rock, his Redeemer, this very psalm that he has written, the product of his pen, the sincere utterance of his mouth, the honest, meditative brooding of his heart. This is his sacrifice, his offering unto God. May God receive both it and him!"[4]

The Word of God is the standard that the Spirit uses to make us aware of our sins. The right way to respond to this conviction of sin is to repent, be forgiven, and live according to the Word. The people who heard Peter preach at Pentecost repented (Acts 2:37-41). Jesus taught that one test of having heard the Word is to obey it (Matt. 7:24-27). James compared those who fail to obey the Word to people who look in the mirror but do nothing about it (Jas. 1:22-25). Not all accept the truth that the Word shows them. Josiah repented when he heard the Word read (2 Kings 22:11-14), but Jehoiakim rejected it and even tried to destroy it (Jer. 36:22-24). When Paul preached in Athens, some believed; but most mocked the message or postponed any decision (Acts 17:32-34).

This is still true. Some hear the Word, are convicted, seek forgiveness, and live according to the Word. Others try to avoid hearing or reading the Word so they never really see themselves as God sees them. Others hear but reject the message.

What are the lasting lessons in Psalm 19:12-14?

1. Pray for discernment to see unintentional sins and be cleansed of them.

2. Pray not to fall into serious intentional sins, which enslave.

3. We are to commit our prayers, thoughts, and meditations to the Lord.

Standard for Salvation (2 Timothy 3:14-15)

*What had Timothy **learned** and who had taught him? Why should children be taught the Bible? How does the written Word of God lead to **salvation**?*

2 Timothy 3:14-15: But continue thou in the things which thou hast learned and hast been assured of, knowing of whom thou hast learned them; ¹⁵and that from a child thou hast known the holy scriptures, which are able to make thee wise unto salvation through faith which is in Christ Jesus.

Paul's close personal relation to Timothy is apparent in these verses. He used the emphatic word for **thou.** In this last letter to Timothy, Paul was like a father giving last-minute instructions to a son leaving for college. Paul repeated many things that he had taught Timothy before, emphasizing the most important things. Paul considered it crucial that Timothy **continue . . . in the things which** he had **learned.** All that Timothy knew about Christ and the Christian way were things he had learned at various times throughout his life, beginning as **a child. Child** is *brephous,* which means "a small child."

Timothy had been taught **the holy scriptures** from the time he was very young. **Holy scriptures** translates *hiera grammata,* which means literally "sacred writings" (NASB, NRSV). This is a different word from the word in verse 16, *graphe,* the usual word for the Scriptures. However, both words refer to the same thing—the Old Testament. Timothy's first teachers were his mother Eunice and his grandmother Lois (1:5). Although Timothy's father was a Greek, no mention is made of his being a believer or teaching Timothy. Eunice was either a widow or she was married to an unbeliever. In spite of these less-than-ideal conditions, she and Lois were faithful in teaching the Word of God to young Timothy.

Probably both Eunice and Timothy became Christians when Paul first preached the good news of Jesus Christ in Lystra (Acts 14:8-20). Timothy's knowledge of the Bible prepared his heart to receive the living Word. Paul's preaching to fellow Jews emphasized that Jesus was the fulfillment of Old Testament promises. What we know for sure from verse 15 is that Timothy's knowledge of the Old Testament made him **wise unto salvation through faith . . . in Christ Jesus.**

The Bible has two main purposes. The first purpose, as shown in this section, is to lead a person to be saved from sin and death through faith in Jesus Christ.

Most of us are indebted to more than one person for teaching us the Bible and leading us to the Lord. When I think back in my life, I realize how many family members, teachers, mentors, friends, and writers have been my teachers. My parents lived a Christian life, shared their faith, and took me to Sunday School. Some of my grandparents influenced me in the faith also. Other family members and some of my friends did their part. My Sunday School teachers and pastors preached and lived for Christ. One or two served as mentors to me. Teachers in college and seminary provided insight and help. Writers such as Elton Trueblood and C. S. Lewis helped me maintain my faith in a skeptical world. Each has played a part in helping me learn the Bible, come to Christ, and live the Christian life.

What are the lasting lessons of 2 Timothy 3:14-15?

1. The Bible should be taught to children.

2. Parents and other mature believers can do their part to teach the Scriptures and lead young ones to Christ.

3. The first purpose of the Holy Scriptures is to lead people to salvation through faith in Jesus Christ.

Standard for Christian Growth (2 Timothy 3:16-17)

How is the inspiration of the Bible unique? What are the four areas of benefits of the Bible in verse 16? What two results of the Bible are in verse 17?

2 Timothy 3:16-17: All scripture is given by inspiration of God, and is profitable for doctrine, for reproof, for correction, for instruction in righteousness: [17]that the man of God may be perfect, thoroughly furnished unto all good works.

These are the most important biblical verses about the Bible itself. The word **scripture** refers to the Old Testament, which was the Bible of the early Christians. The wording allows for two ways of translating the first part of verse 16. Most translations follow the pattern of the *King James Version*: **all scripture is given by inspiration of God.** The other translation possibility reads: "every inspired scripture has its use" (NEB). The latter translation can imply that not all of the Bible is inspired but only the part that is useful for the purposes listed in the rest of the verse. This is not how most of us understand the meaning. Paul was not implying that only part of the Bible is inspired. He was affirming that **all scripture** is inspired. **Inspiration** translates *theopneustos,* which literally means "God-breathed" (NIV). The word for "breath" is the same as the word for "Spirit" *(pneuma).* The Spirit of God is the inspirer of the Bible. **All scripture** for those of Paul's day was the Old Testament, but the good news of Christ took written form and the New Testament is now among that which is **all scripture.**

People sometimes use the word *inspired* of some writing other than the Bible. This general use of the word means that the writing is written with great skill and exerts a powerful impact on readers. This is also true of the Bible, but only the Bible is "God-breathed." Only the Bible is uniquely inspired by God to communicate God's revelation.

The Bible **is profitable** ("useful," NIV) **for doctrine, for reproof, for correction, for instruction in righteousness.** Thus it is our God-given standard for basic areas of Christian doctrine, discipline, and righteous living. The Bible is our handbook for what we believe, how we discipline one another, and how we are to live.

Verse 17 shows that the Bible is also our handbook or standard for Christian service. God gave us the inspired Scriptures **that the man of God may be perfect** ("complete," HCSB; "proficient," NRSV; "adequate," NASB), **thoroughly furnished unto all good works** ("equipped for every good work," NIV). "If Timothy would nurture his spiritual life in the Scriptures that he would use in his ministry, he would be fully qualified and prepared to undertake whatever tasks God put before him. What a tragedy for any Christian to be labeled as spiritually unprepared for a task when the means of instruction and preparation are readily at hand!"[5]

A poll of church members from the nation's 12 largest denominations found that failure to believe the Bible results in false doctrines. Less than half (41 percent) believed in the total accuracy of the Bible. The Barna Research Group took the poll. George Barna concluded: "The Christian body in America is immersed in a crisis of biblical illiteracy. How else can you describe matters when most churchgoing adults reject the accuracy of the Bible, reject the existence of Satan, claim that Jesus sinned, see no need to evangelize, believe that good works are one of the keys to persuading God to forgive their sins, and describe their commitment to Christianity as moderate or even less firm?"[6]

What are the lasting lessons in 2 Timothy 3:16-17?

1. All Scripture is uniquely inspired by God.

2. The second purpose of the Bible is for believers' growth. The Bible is the standard for doctrine, discipline, godly living, and Christian service.

❖ *Spiritual Transformations*

God inspired both the Old Testament and the New Testament. The Bible is a perfect standard that reveals sins and points to God's offer of forgiveness of sins. The first purpose of the Bible is to lead us to salvation through faith in Jesus Christ. Then the Bible becomes the standard and guide for doctrine, discipline, Christian living, and Christian service.

The comments on the Bible mention two polls: one on morality and the other on doctrine. If you had been one of those answering the poll, how would you have answered questions about your moral standards and practices and about your doctrinal beliefs, especially your belief in the Bible? The real test of both areas, however, is how we actually live. Many give nonbiblical answers. More disturbing are those who claim to believe the Bible and its standards for beliefs and morals but who live as though they do not believe these standards. The Life Impact of this lesson is to help you live by biblical standards, not just to profess to believe them.

In what ways is the Bible a standard for what you believe and how you live? _____

How much of what you do in daily life is determined by biblical standards? _____

Prayer of Commitment: Lord, help me to live by the standards of Your inspired Word. Amen.

[1]Elmer A. Leslie, *The Psalms* [Nashville: Abingdon Press, 1949], 174.

[2]"Barna Poll on Morality Uncovers Troubling Trends," *Baptist and Reflector*, October 3, 2001, 2.

[3]F. Delitzsch, *Exposition of the Psalms*, vol. 1, of *Psalms*, in *Commentary on the Old Testament*, vol. V, by C. F. Keil and F. Delitzsch [Grand Rapids: William B. Eerdmans Publishing Company, 1991 reprint of 1871 edition], 288.

[4]Leslie, *The Psalms*, 175.

[5]Thomas D. Lea, "1, 2 Timothy, Titus," in *The New American Commentary*, vol. 34 [Nashville: Broadman Press, 1992], 237-238.

[6]"Baptists, Others Adrift in Doctrinal Beliefs," *Baptist and Reflector*, August 22, 2001, 8.

THE BIBLE: ITS TESTIMONY

Background Passage: John 5:31-47; Acts 17:1-15
Focal Passage: John 5:37-40,45-47; Acts 17:2-4,11-12
Key Verse: John 5:39

❖ *Significance of the Lesson*

• The *Theme* of this lesson is that all Scripture is a testimony to Christ, who is Himself the focus of divine revelation.
• The *Life Question* addressed in this lesson is, What does the Bible teach me?
• The *Biblical Theme* is that the Scriptures testify about Jesus.
• The *Life Impact* is to help you regularly study the Scriptures to learn about and follow Jesus.

Jesus and the Bible

Non-Christian worldviews do not see Jesus as the focus of the Bible. Secular worldviews ignore or reject the Bible and the Lord of whom it speaks.

The biblical worldview sees the Bible as a testimony to Jesus Christ, who is the focus of the message of the Bible.

Word Study: *borne witness, testify*

The Greek word *martureo* means "to bear witness" to something or someone or "to testify" on behalf of someone. The noun form is *marturia,* "testimony." Both words are found many times in John 5: 31-39. This passage lists those who bore witness or testimony to Jesus.

❖ *Search the Scriptures*

Jesus taught that the Scriptures bore witness to Him as God's Son. Paul and the other apostles preached the death and resurrection of Jesus as the focus of the Scriptures. The Bereans examined the

Scriptures with open minds, eagerly, and daily. Some Jews and Greeks believed the preaching of the good news, but others rejected Jesus.

The four points of the outline present why and how people should study the Bible to learn about and follow Jesus.

Testimony of the Scriptures (John 5:37-40,45-47)

How did God bear witness that Jesus was His Son? What three areas of the Pharisees' ignorance did Jesus mention? Why did the Pharisees search the Scriptures? Why did they not find what they sought? What was the tragic irony of the Pharisees' emphasis on Moses?

John 5:37-40: **And the Father himself, which hath sent me, hath borne witness of me. Ye have neither heard his voice at anytime, nor seen his shape. [38]And ye have not his word abiding in you: for whom he hath sent, him ye believe not. [39]Search the scriptures; for in them ye think ye have eternal life: and they are they which testify of me. [40]And ye will not come to me, that ye might have life.**

John 5 begins with Jesus' healing a sick man on the Sabbath; for which the Pharisees criticized Him and even sought to kill Him (vv. 1-18). Jesus responded by emphasizing the marks of His Sonship to God (vv. 19-30). Then Jesus supported this claim by listing those who bore witness to Him. He mentioned John the Baptist (vv. 31-35). Jesus said that God bore witness to Him through the miracles He did (v. 36). God bore witness to Jesus in other ways. As Jesus put it, **The Father himself, which hath sent me, hath borne witness of me.**

Jesus' critics did not respond positively to this testimony of the Father to the Son. "Their ignorance is threefold. (i) They have never heard God's voice. Moses heard that voice (Ex. 33:11), but they are no true followers of Moses, otherwise they would have heard God's voice in Jesus (3:34; 17:8). (ii) They have never seen God's form. Israel saw that form (Gen. 32:30f.), but they are no true Israelites. Were they, they would have seen God in Jesus (14:9). (iii) They have not God's word abiding in them. The Psalmist laid up God's word in his heart (Ps. 119:11), but they do not share his religious experience. Had they done so they would have received that word from Jesus (17:14)."[1]

Jesus spoke plainly in explaining His critics' plight: **him ye believe not** ("you do not believe the one he sent," NIV). In other words, they did not believe the Father's testimony to His Son because they did not believe the Son.

In **search the scriptures, search** (*eraunate*) can be indicative ("you search," NKJV; NASB; NRSV; similarly, NIV and HCSB) or imperative. If it is an imperative, Jesus was telling them to **search the scriptures.** This assumes that the Pharisees needed to study the Scriptures. Verses 39-40, however, seem to indicate that they knew the Bible. Their problem was not failure to study the Bible; it was their failure to see the written Word as a testimony to the living Word. Most people who reject Jesus are largely ignorant of the Bible, but some who know much about the Bible still reject the One to whom it bears witness.

The Pharisees studied the Bible because they believed that it contained the way of **eternal life.** They were right about this, but when confronted by the One who is the way, they rejected Him. "You diligently study the Scriptures because you think that by them you possess eternal life. These are the Scriptures that testify about me, yet you refuse to come to me to have life" (NIV). Jesus' words emphasize the irony of their actions. The Pharisees were looking for eternal life. They believed that the way to life was in the Bible; thus they searched the Scriptures. But when they saw Jesus, the way to life, they rejected Him and thus missed the very life they were seeking.

John 5:45-47: **Do not think that I will accuse you to the Father: there is one that accuseth you, even Moses, in whom ye trust. ⁴⁶For had ye believed Moses, ye would have believed me: for he wrote of me. ⁴⁷But if ye believe not his writings, how shall ye believe my words?**

The Pharisees held **Moses** in high regard. They considered themselves "Moses' disciples" (9:28). They emphasized the law as the way of life, and they honored Moses as the one through whom God gave the law. They placed their **trust** ("hopes," NIV) in Moses. Imagine their surprise when Jesus told them that He was not the one who accused them. He said, "Do not think that I will accuse you before the Father. Your accuser is Moses, on whom your hopes are set" (NIV).

In what sense was Moses their accuser? Jesus explained that Moses **wrote** of Jesus. Thus if they truly **believed** Moses, they **would have believed** Jesus, of whom Moses wrote. Jesus asked, **If ye believe not his writings, how shall ye believe my words?**

The Bible points people to Jesus Christ as the Son of God and Savior of the world. After Jesus' resurrection, Luke 24:44 describes how Jesus told the disciples that He fulfilled all three divisions of the Old Testament—Law, Prophets, and Writings (Psalms is the longest book in this division). The Four Gospels tell the heart of His story, and the rest of the New Testament interprets the mind of Christ. Christians believe that people who let God's Word speak to them will be confronted with Jesus and the need to commit to Him. If studying the Bible does not lead to Jesus, the students have missed its main point.

How can anyone study the Bible and still reject Jesus Christ? Peter wrote of people who twist the Scriptures to their own destruction (2 Pet. 3:16). The religious leaders in John 5:16-17 had criticized Jesus for healing on the Sabbath. This rule, however, is not from the Bible but from their own set of rules about keeping the Fourth Commandment. They studied the Scriptures, but they saw the Word of God through the lens of human traditions.

What people today search the Scriptures but do not believe in Jesus? Some study the Bible purely for its literary value. The Bible is great literature, but it is far more. People who see it only as great literature fail to see its real message, which centers in Jesus. Some people study the Bible only for its historical value. It is one of the primary sources for life in ancient times, but it is far more. The Bible contains true history, but it is more than history; it is *His Story*. Some people study the Bible to find fault with it or with the Christian faith. Some of those who study the Bible for the wrong reasons become convicted of their sins and become followers of Jesus. Others are like Jesus' critics, whose hearts are hardened against the truth.

Many people do not know Jesus because they do not know the Scriptures. Several years ago some graduate students were watching a football game on television. A shot of the end zone revealed a sign reading "John 3:16." One student asked what the sign meant. One said he thought it was a Bible verse, but only one of them knew the verse and what it meant. That student told the others about the verse and its meaning.

The same student worked in a lab with about a dozen other well-educated people. The student asked them how many of them knew John 3:16. Two did; the others did not. He shared the verse with them. No wonder so many people do not know Jesus if our best educated people do not know John 3:16!

What are the lasting lessons in John 5:37-40,45-47?

1. In the Holy Scriptures God bears witness to Jesus as His Son.

2. Many people miss Jesus because they neglect or reject the Bible; but some study the Bible without seeing Jesus as its key message. Either way, those people miss the life that only Jesus can offer.

3. A professed love and reverence for the Bible is proven to be false if Jesus is not believed. The Bible itself condemns those who reject Jesus.

Focus of the Scriptures (Acts 17:2-3)

Where was Paul? What was his message? How was it presented?
Acts 17:2-3: **And Paul, as his manner was, went in unto them, and three sabbath days reasoned with them out of the scriptures, [3]opening and alleging, that Christ must needs have suffered, and risen again from the dead; and that this Jesus, whom I preach unto you, is Christ.**

These events took place on Paul's second missionary journey. Paul had heard and responded to the Macedonian call (Acts 16:9-10). He went to Philippi, where he won to Christ at least three persons: Lydia, a slave girl, and the jailer (vv. 12-40). Passing through two other cities, he came to Thessalonica, the capital of the Roman province of Macedonia. In the city was a Jewish synagogue.

Paul's missionary strategy was to go to the synagogue first. There he found people who revered the Scriptures and were looking for the Messiah. Paul was able to use their Scriptures to show that Jesus is the Messiah **(Christ).** This usual approach was followed in the synagogue in Thessalonica. For **three sabbath days,** Paul **reasoned with them out of the scriptures. Reasoned** is one of four words used to describe what Paul did. **Opening and alleging** can be translated "explaining" (NIV) and "showing" (HCSB). **Preach** is a common word in the New Testament for proclaiming a message. In other words, Paul used every form of preaching and teaching to declare his message.

What was the message? Verse 3 says that it was **that Christ must needs have suffered, and risen again from the dead; and that this Jesus . . . is Christ.** The Bible points to Jesus and focuses our attention on His death and His resurrection. The sermons of Peter and Paul bear this out. Peter preached this twofold gospel at Pentecost (2:22-36). He did the same thing in later messages (3:15), including the message to Cornelius and his family (10:37-43). Paul did the same thing at the synagogue in Antioch of Pisidia (13:26-38). He followed the same pattern at Thessalonica. When he summed up the message of the gospel for the Corinthians, he wrote how he preached: "that Christ died for our sins according to the scriptures; and that he was buried, and that he rose again the third day according to the scriptures" (1 Cor. 15:3-4).

Must needs means "had to" (NIV). Jesus was under a moral obligation to suffer. He was not forced to die; indeed He could have chosen not to suffer and die on the cross. He was innocent and sinless. The necessity came from the needs of a lost sinful world. He had to die for salvation to be made possible.

Jesus tried to teach the disciples of this mission, but they did not understand because they were looking for a powerful, victorious king as their messiah. Only after His resurrection did the apostles see the necessity of the cross and resurrection as God's victory over sin and death. When they preached the crucified, risen Lord to the ancient world, they often met ridicule and rejection. The cross was a stumbling block for Jews and foolishness to the Greeks (1 Cor. 1:18-19). The Greeks and Romans laughed at the idea of resurrection of the body (Acts 17:32). But for the saved, then and now, the heart of the good news is the death of Jesus for our sins and His victory over death on our behalf.

No wonder some of our most popular Christian music focuses on the cross and resurrection.

> When I survey the wondrous cross,
> On which the Prince of glory died,
> My richest gain I count but loss,
> And pour contempt on all my pride.[2]

And again:

> Because He lives I can face tomorrow;
> Because He lives all fear is gone;
> Because I know He holds the future,
> And life is worth the living just because He lives.[3]

What are the lasting lessons of Acts 17:2-3?

1. Use every means of communication to present the good news.
2. Focus on the death and resurrection of Jesus.

Examination of the Scriptures (Acts 17:11)

Why are the Bereans held up as a good example? What words describe them and how they dealt with the Bible?

Acts 17:11: **These were more noble than those in Thessalonica, in that they received the word with all readiness of mind, and searched the scriptures daily, whether those things were so.**

After Paul had preached for three weeks in Thessalonica, his enemies started a riot protesting the work of the Christian missionaries.

Some of those in the synagogue were jealous of Paul's success. Paul and Silas were forced to leave town (vv. 5-9). They made their way to Berea, and they did what they had done in Thessalonica. That is, they preached Christ in the synagogue. However, the Bereans responded differently from the people of Thessalonica. The word translated **more noble** is *eugenesteroi.* This word "originally meant *high born* but came to have a more general connotation of being open, tolerant, generous, having the qualities that go with 'good breeding.'"[4] The translations vary: "more noble character" (NIV), "more noble-minded" (NASB), "more open-minded" (HCSB), "more receptive" (NRSV), "more civil" (NEB), and "more fair-minded" (REB).

The opposite response to the openness of the Bereans is to hear with closed minds and hearts. Paul often encountered this attitude, just as Jesus had in John 5:39-40. Some people come to the Bible with their minds already made up and their opinions already formed. If the Bible does not agree with their views, they go with their views instead of making the changes the Word of God calls for. The Bereans had not heard the message that Jesus was the Messiah, but they listened with open hearts to what Paul said. Then they eagerly studied the Scriptures to see if what Paul said was true.

Four other phrases describe the way the Bereans responded. First, **they received the word. Received** translates *edexanto,* which can mean "welcomed" (HCSB). Some people hear the Word of God, but do so reluctantly. They do their best to avoid being confronted by the message of the Scriptures. When they cannot escape it, they listen reluctantly.

Second, **all readiness of mind** is usually translated "great eagerness" (NIV). The Bereans were excited by what they heard Paul say, and they were eager to conduct further study to determine the truth of what he said. The opposite of eagerness is indifference. Too many people are indifferent toward the Word of God.

Third, **searched** is a different word from the word in John 5:39. Paul's word *anakrinontes* means "examining" (NASB) or "studying" (NEB, REB). The Bereans did not look at the Bible superficially, but they dug deeply into it as they sought to find the truth. They did what is sometimes called "in-depth Bible study." This takes time, effort, intelligence, and the full use of all available helps.

Fourth, they not only heard the message of Paul on the Sabbath, but they also studied the Word of God **daily.** This involved personal Bible study and probably also small-group study.

The Bereans are a good model not only for those who are seeking the Lord for the first time but also for disciples of the Lord. How many different opportunities of Bible study do you have? How many of these are a regular part of your life? Here are some opportunities that most of us have. We have the opportunity to prepare for and participate in Bible study in Sunday School. Many miss this basic opportunity by not attending weekly Bible study in an adult class. Many who attend have not studied their lesson and thus are not equipped to participate. We have opportunities to listen with open Bibles when the pastor preaches. We have the freedom to read and study the Bible each day. The quarterly or lesson guidebooks provide suggestions for daily Bible readings for each adult and suggestions for family Bible study. The Bereans would have taken advantage of all such opportunities.

What are the lasting lessons of Acts 17:11?

1. People should receive God's Word with open minds and hearts.
2. Those who do this welcome the Word with eagerness.
3. Such persons study God's Word on the Lord's Day and each day.

Goal of the Scriptures (Acts 17:4,12)

What groups heard the gospel in Thessalonica and in Berea? How did the people respond?

Acts 17:4,12: And some of them believed, and consorted with Paul and Silas; and of the devout Greeks a great multitude, and of the chief women not a few.

. . . .

[12]Therefore many of them believed; also of honorable women which were Greeks, and of men, not a few.

One reason Paul preached in the synagogues was to begin with people who claimed to believe the same Scriptures he believed and who were looking for the Messiah. In this group, of course, were not only Jews but also **devout Greeks.** This group often is called "God-fearing Greeks" (NIV). These were Gentiles who believed in the God of Israel and in the Scriptures. The Ethiopian eunuch of 8:26-40 and Cornelius of 10:1–11:18 seem to have been such people. They were not yet proselytes who had become converts to Judaism; but in most synagogues there were also some men who had been circumcised and came under the covenant as a convert. In the synagogue were both **men** and **women.**

Among those who heard and responded positively in both cities were many **chief women** or **honorable women.** These "prominent women" (NIV) show that in that part of Greece some women were highly regarded in society. Lydia was a prominent woman in nearby Philippi. She seems to have had her own business and opened her home as a meeting place for the church (16:14-15,40).

Verse 4 describes the initial response in Thessalonica. **Some of them** (apparently of the Jews) responded positively and **believed.** But **of the devout Greeks a great multitude, and of the chief women not a few,** responded positively. More of all groups believed in Berea, including more of the Jews themselves. The response of so many Greeks who had been attending the synagogue in Thessalonica explains why the Jewish leaders became jealous of Paul (v. 5).

Verse 4 also tells us what positive response was made. They **believed** and **consorted with Paul and Silas.** The word translated **believed** in verse 4 means "were persuaded." In verse 12, **believed** is the usual word for saving faith. **Consorted with** is a word that means "joined" (NIV). In other words, the believers who joined with Paul and Silas became the nucleus of the church. Paul's policy was to evangelize and to form churches. The New Testament knows nothing of believers who do not become part of a church.

What are the lasting lessons in Acts 17:4,12?

1. All people need to hear the good news of the Scriptures. But the responses vary.

2. Those who hear the good news should believe and join the church.

Emile Cailliet grew up in France in the early years of the 20th century. During his college years he was an agnostic. He had never seen a Bible. He was wounded in World War I and barely escaped death. After the war he began to search for something meaningful in life. He loved to read and occasionally found something that seemed to speak to him. He carefully copied such passages in a leather-bound book. He expected this to become what he called "a book that would understand me." Finally he finished his book and sat down under a tree to read it. He expected to find guidance for life. However, as he continued to read, he felt growing disappointment. He realized that the whole project would not work because he had put it together, the book was of his own making.

On that same day his wife went walking and found herself in a place where she had never been before. It turned out to be a Huguenot (French Protestant) Church. She met the pastor and asked for a Bible.

Returning home she told her husband what had happened. Instead of being angry, he asked to see the Bible. Here is how he described what happened then: "She complied. I literally grabbed the book and rushed to my study with it. I opened it and 'chanced' upon the Beatitudes! I read, and read, and read—now aloud with an undescribable warmth surging within . . . I could not find words to express my awe and wonder. And all of a sudden, the realization dawned upon me: This *was* 'the book that would understand me.' I needed it so much that I had attempted to write my own—in vain. I continued to read deep into the night, mostly from the Gospels. And lo and behold, as I looked *through* them, the One of whom they spoke, the One who spoke and acted in them, became alive in me."[5]

❖ *Spiritual Transformations*

Those who study the Bible but reject Jesus miss the life Jesus alone can give. The Bible points to Him. The focus of the good news in the Bible is the death of Jesus and His resurrection from the dead. People need to carefully examine the Bible eagerly and daily. Those who hear the good news should believe the message and join a Bible-believing church.

The Life Impact of this lesson is to help you regularly study the Scriptures to learn about and follow Jesus. How many of the following statements are true of you?

◘ *I have trusted Jesus as my Savior and participate in the life of a Bible-believing church.*

◘ *I listen and obey God's Word as proclaimed and taught in His church.*

◘ *I regularly prepare for and participate in a Sunday School class.*

◘ *I study the Bible daily.*

Prayer of Commitment: Lord, help me to grow in Your Word as I learn more about Jesus and follow Him more closely. Amen.

[1]Leon Morris, *The Gospel According to John*, in The New International Commentary on the New Testament [Grand Rapids: William B. Eerdmans Publishing Company, 1971], 329.

[2]Isaac Watts, "When I Survey the Wondrous Cross," No. 144, *The Baptist Hymnal*, 1991.

[3]Gloria and William J. Gaither, "Because He Lives," No. 407, *The Baptist Hymnal*, 1991.

[4]John B. Polhill, "Acts," in *The New American Commentary*, vol. 26 [Nashville: Broadman Press, 1992], 363.

[5]Emile Cailliet, "The Book that Understands Me," *Christianity Today*, November 22, 1963, 10-11.